Writing about Literature
A Portable Guide

Writing about Literature

A Portable Guide

Second Edition

JANET E. GARDNER

University of Massachusetts at Dartmouth

Bedford/St. Martin's   BOSTON ◆ NEW YORK

For Bedford/St. Martin's

Executive Editor: Stephen A. Scipione
Production Editor: Annette Pagliaro Sweeney
Production Supervisor: Sarah Ulicny
Marketing Manager: Adrienne Petsick
Editorial Assistant: Marisa Feinstein
Copyeditor: Jan Cocker
Text Design: Sandra Rigney
Cover Design: Donna Lee Dennison
Composition: TexTech International
Printing and Binding: Haddon Craftsmen, Inc., an RR Donnelley &
Sons Company

President: Joan E. Feinberg
Editorial Director: Denise B. Wydra
Editor in Chief: Karen S. Henry
Director of Marketing: Karen R. Soeltz
Director of Editing, Design, and Production: Marcia Cohen
Assistant Director of Editing, Design, and Production: Elise S. Kaiser
Managing Editor: Elizabeth M. Schaaf

Library of Congress Control Number: 2008925876

Manufactured in the United States of America

3 2 1
k j i h g

For information, write: Bedford/St. Martin's, 75 Arlington Street,
Boston, MA 02116 (617-399-4000)

ISBN-10: 0–312–60757-1
ISBN-13: 978–0–312–60757-9

Preface

This book is designed to help students in literature classes master the sometimes daunting task of writing effective critical papers and is intended to be used alongside individual literary texts or any anthology lacking substantial writing instruction. It grows out of my years in the classroom working with students from diverse backgrounds and with a variety of skill levels. The text is brief and accessible enough for students to read on their own, without taking too much vital time from the central task of reading and exploring literature. It presents reading, writing, research, and critical thinking as interrelated and mutually supporting skills.

The opening chapter on the role of good reading shows students how to move beyond the basics of decoding and initial comprehension by emphasizing the interpretive nature of critical reading. Students are directed, through concrete examples and specific instructions, to take a more active approach to reading than many of them have taken in the past. The chapter encourages textual annotation, note taking, journal keeping, and, above all, the crucial practice of asking questions and approaching the act of reading literature as a collaborative process between author and reader. Students should come away from this chapter more confident that their ideas and responses are a valid and necessary part of understanding literature.

The subsequent chapters devoted specifically to writing instruction further integrate critical reading strategies as they cover the entire writing process from topic choice through proofreading and finalizing manuscript format. Substantial attention is paid to developing an original thesis and supporting that thesis with specific evidence from the primary text as well as other sources. Separate chapters address specific issues related to thinking and writing about short fiction, poetry, and drama, and students are also introduced to some of the most common sorts of writing assignments and several critical theories most useful to their examination of literary texts.

Throughout the book, critical thinking plays a central role, and nowhere is this more apparent than in Chapter 7, devoted to research. Here, the nuts and bolts of library research and MLA documentation are presented in the context of true research — the sort of critical search and synthesis that allows us to satisfy our own curiosity while contributing to the understanding of our readers. To help make these lessons more concrete to students, the book also includes a sampling of literary texts for analysis and several student papers modeling a variety of approaches and styles. Terms commonly used in literature classes appear in **boldface** throughout the text and are indexed for ease of reference at the back of the book. My hope is that this brief guide will help students increase their understanding of literature and more fully appreciate the intellectual challenges and personal rewards inherent in taking responsibility for their own responses to their reading, in their literature class and beyond.

NEW TO THE SECOND EDITION

The second edition includes more brief examples of literature and specific responses to those examples. Several models of critical reading and writing have been added. For example, Chapter 1 includes Samuel Taylor Coleridge's "Kubla Khan" and a student's annotations of the poem that raise questions about the text and point to possible writing topics. Chapter 3 now includes three new poems, and features three new student papers — an explication, an analysis, and a comparison-contrast paper — that respond to the poems. Also, the discussion of the elements of poetry in Chapter 5 has been substantially revised and expanded to include more elements and more examples of them. In Chapter 7, more models of MLA documentation style have been included. Throughout, I have added summary checklists that students can quickly consult when they undertake their critical reading and writing about literature.

A NOTE ON MLA DOCUMENTATION

As you may know, the Modern Language Association publishes two versions of its guidelines for documenting sources. The *MLA Style Manual and Guide to Scholarly Publishing* is for scholars and graduate students. The *MLA Handbook for Writers of Research Papers* is for undergraduate and high school students. In May 2008, the guide for scholars was updated with new guidelines for documenting sources. The Modern Language Association strongly discouraged publishers from updating texts intended for undergraduates to reflect the changes in the scholars' guide. Accordingly, the coverage of MLA documentation in *Writing about Literature* reflects the guidelines for undergraduates as put forth in the current edition of the *MLA Handbook for Writers of Research Papers*. When the Modern Language Association publishes the new edition of this guide (anticipated in the spring of 2009), student copies of *Writing about Literature* will be reprinted to reflect these new guidelines.

ACKNOWLEDGEMENTS

I am, of course, deeply grateful to the many people who were instrumental in helping me with the creation of this book. Among the many people at Bedford/St. Martin's who deserve special thanks are Joan Feinberg and Elizabeth Schaaf. Steve Scipione was, as ever, supportive and critical in equal measure, helping to shape this volume into the best pedagogical tool it could be. Marisa Feinstein efficiently conducted the review program and kept things moving along in her role as editorial assistant, assembling the manuscript and filling holes and gaps. Production editor Annette Pagliaro Sweeney kept the project running smoothly, coordinating a myriad of details. Joanne Diaz made indispensable contributions to the revision; without her, this second edition would not exist. I owe personal thanks as well to those who helped shape my own love of reading, writing, and teaching about literature—including the many fine teachers and colleagues I have encountered over the years and, especially, my students. Special thanks are also due to Sarah Johnson, a fine writer and a precious friend, and to Pat McCorkle for his editorial acumen and his unflagging support.

Contents

Writing about
Literature
A Portable Guide

Introduction
Writing about Literature

Some students really enjoy reading imaginative literature and writing papers about it, while others find the task intimidating, frustrating, or just plain dull. If you're in the first group, you're lucky; your literature class will be fun and interesting for you, and — not incidentally — you'll probably do good work in the course. If you've never been fond of reading and writing about literature, though, you might spend a little time thinking about why some of your classmates enjoy this sort of work as well as what you might do to increase your own enjoyment of literature and investment in the writing process. You'll be happier and write better papers if you can put aside any previous negative experiences with literature and writing you may have had and approach your task with a positive mindset.

So let's take a moment to reflect on why we read and write about literature. Of course, there is no single or simple answer. People read to be informed, to be entertained, to be exposed to new ideas, or to have familiar concepts reinforced. Often, people read just to enjoy a good story or to get a glimpse of how other people think and feel. But literature does much more than give us a compelling plot or a look into an author's thoughts and emotions — although at its best it does these things as well. Literature explores the larger world and the ways in which people interact with that world and with one another. So even when what we read is entirely fictional, we nevertheless learn about real life. And, indeed, by affecting our thoughts and feelings, literature can indirectly affect our actions as well. Thus literature not only reflects but even helps to shape our world.

Writing about literature also has real-world usefulness. By forcing us to organize our thoughts and state clearly what we think, writing an essay helps us to clarify what we know and believe. It gives us a chance to affect the thinking of our readers. Even more important, we actually learn as we write. In the process of writing, we often make new discoveries and forge new connections between ideas. We find and work through contradictions in our thinking, and we create whole new lines of thought as we work to make linear sense out of an often chaotic jumble of impressions. So, while *reading* literature can teach us much about the world, *writing* about literature often teaches us about ourselves.

1

CHAPTER 1

The Role of Good Reading

Writing about literature begins, of course, with reading, so it stands to reason that good reading is the first step toward successful writing. But what exactly is "good reading"? Good reading is, generally speaking, not fast reading. In fact, often the best advice a student can receive about reading is to *slow down*. Reading well is all about paying attention, and you can't pay attention if you're racing to get through an assignment and move on to "more important" things. If you make a point of giving yourself plenty of time and minimizing your distractions, you'll get more out of your reading and probably enjoy it more as well.

THE VALUE OF REREADING

An important thing to remember is that the best reading is often rereading. The best readers are those who are willing to go back and reread a piece of literature again and again. It is not uncommon for professional literary critics—who are, after all, some of the most skilled readers—to read a particular poem, story, or play literally dozens of times before they feel equipped to write about it. And well-written literature rewards this willingness to reread, allowing readers to continue seeing new things with each reading. Realistically, of course, you will not have the time to read every assigned piece many times before discussing it in class or preparing to write about it, but you should not give up or feel frustrated if you fail to "get" a piece of literature on the first reading. Be prepared to go back and reread key sections, or even a whole work, if doing so could help with your understanding.

CRITICAL READING

What we are trying to encourage is what is sometimes called "active reading" or "critical reading," though *critical* here implies not fault-finding but rather thoughtful consideration. Much of the reading we do in everyday life is passive and noncritical. We glance at street signs to see where we are; we check the sports section to find out how our favorite team is doing in the standings; we read packages for information about the products we use. And in general, we take in all this information passively, without questioning it or looking for deeper meaning. For many kinds of reading, this is perfectly appropriate. It would hardly make sense to ask, "*Why* is this Pine Street?" or "What do they *mean* when they say there are 12 ounces of soda in this can?" There is, however, another type of reading, one that involves asking critical questions and probing more deeply into the meaning of what we read, and this is the kind of reading most appropriate to imaginative literature (especially if we intend to discuss or write about that literature later).

THE MYTH OF "HIDDEN MEANING"

There is a persistent myth in literature classes that the purpose of reading is to scour a text for "hidden meaning." Do not be taken in by this myth. In fact, many instructors dislike the phrase *hidden meaning*, which has unpleasant and inaccurate connotations. First, it suggests a sort of willful subterfuge on the part of the author, a deliberate attempt to make his or her work difficult to understand or to exclude the reader. Second, it makes the process of reading sound like digging for buried treasure rather than a systematic intellectual process. Finally, the phrase implies that there is a single, true meaning to a text and that communication and understanding move in one direction only: from the crafty author to the searching reader.

In truth, the meanings in literary texts are not hidden, and your job as a reader is not to root around for them. Rather, if a text is not immediately accessible to you, it is because you need to read more actively, and meaning will then emerge in a collaborative effort as you work *with* the text to create a consistent interpretation. Obviously, this requires effort. If you find this sort of reading hard, take that as a good sign. It means you're paying the sort of attention that a well-crafted poem, story, or play requires of a reader. You also should not assume that English teachers have a key that allows them to unlock the one secret truth of a text. If, as is often the case, your instructor sees more or different meanings in a piece of literature than you do, this is because he or she is trained to read actively and has probably spent much more time than you have with literature in general and more time with the particular text assigned to you.

ACTIVE READING

Annotating

If the first suggestions for active reading are to slow down and to know that a second (or even a third) reading is in order, the next suggestion is to read with a pen or pencil in hand in order to annotate your text and take notes. If you look inside a literature textbook belonging to your instructor or to an advanced literature student, chances are you'll see something of a mess—words and passages circled or underlined, comments and questions scrawled in the margins (technically called *marginalia*) or even between the lines (called *interlinear* notes), and unexplained punctuation marks or other symbols decorating the pages. You should not interpret this as disrespect for the text or author or as a sign of a disordered mind. Indeed, it is quite the opposite of both these things. It is simply textual annotation, and it means that someone has been engaged in active reading. (The poet and critic Samuel Taylor Coleridge was famous for annotating not only his own books but those he borrowed from friends—a habit unlikely to secure a friendship—and his marginalia actually make up one entire volume of his collected works.)

If you are not accustomed to textual annotation, it may be hard to know where to begin. There is no single, widely used system of annotation, and you will almost certainly begin to develop your own techniques as you practice active reading. Here, however, are a few tips to get you started:

- **Underline, circle, or otherwise highlight passages that strike you as particularly important.** These may be anything from single words to whole paragraphs—but stick to those points in the text that really stand out, the briefer and more specific, the better. Don't worry that you need to find *the* most crucial parts of a poem, play, or story. Everyone sees things a little differently, so just note what makes an impression on *you*.

- **Make notes in the margins as to *why* certain points strike you.** Don't just underline; jot down at least a word or two in the margin to remind yourself what you were thinking when you chose to highlight a particular point. It may seem obvious to you at the moment, but when you return to the text in two weeks to write your paper, you may not remember.

- **Ask questions of the text.** Perhaps the most important aspect of active reading is the practice of asking critical questions of a text.

Nobody—not even the most experienced literary critic—understands everything about a literary text immediately, and noting where you are confused or doubtful is an important first step toward resolving any confusion. We discuss types of questions a little later in this chapter, but for now just remember that any point of confusion is fair game, from character **motivation** (*"Why would she do that?"*), to cultural or historical references (*"Where is Xanadu?"*), to the definitions of individual words (*"Meaning?"*). Most likely, you will eventually want to propose some possible answers, but on a first reading of the text, it's enough to note that you have questions.

- **Talk back to the text.** Occasionally, something in a literary text may strike you as suspicious, offensive, or just plain wrong. Just because a story, poem, or play appears in a textbook does not make its author above criticism. Try to keep an open mind and realize that there may be an explanation that would satisfy your criticism, but if you think an author has made a misstep, don't be afraid to make note of your opinion.

- **Look for unusual features of language.** In creating a mood and making a point, literary works rely much more heavily than do purely informational texts on features of language such as style and imagery. As a reader of literature, then, you need to heighten your awareness of style. Look for patterns of images, repeated words or phrases, and any other unusual stylistic features—right down to idiosyncratic grammar or punctuation—and make note of them in your marginalia.

- **Develop your own system of shorthand.** Annotating a text, while it obviously takes time, shouldn't become a burden or slow your reading too much, so keep your notes and questions short and to the point. Sometimes all you need is an exclamation point to indicate an important passage. An underlined term combined with a question mark in the margin can remind you that you didn't immediately understand what a word meant. Be creative, but try also to be consistent, so you'll know later what you meant by a particular symbol or comment.

A student decided to write her paper on Samuel Taylor Coleridge's "Kubla Khan." Here are some of the annotations that she made as she read the poem:

SAMUEL TAYLOR COLERIDGE   [1772–1834]

Kubla Khan

In Xanadu did Kubla Khan
A stately pleasure dome decree:
Where Alph, the sacred river, ran
Through caverns measureless to man
   Down to a sunless sea.   5
So twice five miles of fertile ground
With walls and towers were girdled round:
And there were gardens bright with sinuous rills,
Where blossomed many an incense-bearing tree;
And here were forests ancient as the hills,   10
Enfolding sunny spots of greenery.

But oh! that deep romantic chasm which slanted
Down the green hill athwart a cedarn cover!
A savage place! as holy and enchanted
As e'er beneath a waning moon was haunted   15
By woman wailing for her demon lover!
And from this chasm, with ceaseless turmoil seething,
As if this earth in fast thick pants were breathing,
A mighty fountain momently was forced:
Amid whose swift half-intermitted burst   20
Huge fragments vaulted like rebounding hail,
Or chaffy grain beneath the thresher's flail:
And 'mid these dancing rocks at once and ever
It flung up momently the sacred river.
Five miles meandering with a mazy motion   25
Through wood and dale the sacred river ran,
Then reached the caverns measureless to man,
And sank in tumult to a lifeless ocean:
And 'mid this tumult Kubla heard from far
Ancestral voices prophesying war!   30
   The shadow of the dome of pleasure
   Floated midway on the waves;
   Where was heard the mingled measure
   From the fountain and the caves.
It was a miracle of rare device,   35
A sunny pleasure dome with caves of ice!

Genghis Khan's grandson. Britann
Online says he was the first empe
of the Mongol dynasty. Why is he
subject of the poem? An interest
Asia?

Alph?

Sinuous = complex, w
Rills = brooks

The poem starts off
tetrameter (4 pulses
line) then goes to pe
tameter (5 pulses pe
Why does he do that

These stanzas have
11 syllables per line.
Why does he
keep adding
more to each
line? What does it d
the tone of the poe
?

The poem sets up
exact distances. In s
there were "twice five
fertile ground"; in sta
the river is five miles

More repetition: thee
repeat the ends of li
in stanza 1.

Then he goes from pentame
to tetrameter again,
as if bringing the poem
under control.

A damsel with a dulcimer
In a vision once I saw:
It was an Abyssinian maid,
And on her dulcimer she played,
Singing of Mount Abora.   40
Could I revive within me
Her symphony and song,
    To such a deep delight 'twould win me,
That with music loud and long,   45
I would build that dome in air,
That sunny dome! those caves of ice!
And all who heard should see them there,
And all should cry, Beware! Beware!
His flashing eyes, his floating hair!   50
Weave a circle round him thrice,
And close your eyes with holy dread,
For he on honey-dew hath fed,
And drunk the milk of Paradise.

He inverts the syntax numerous times in the poem. Here, does he do it to place more emphasis on the vision of the damsel than on himself?

The poem travels from Kubla Khan (Mongolia/China) to an Abyssinian maid (Eastern Africa).

The exclamation points create a sense of wonder, breathlessness. The repetition of "caves of ice" from stanza 2 makes the speaker sound like he's in some kind of spell.

Notetaking

It's a good idea, especially if you are reading a difficult text or one about which you expect to be writing, to keep a notebook handy as you read, a place to make notes that would be too long or complex to fit in the margins. You might even want to use the same notebook you keep with you in class, so you can make quick reference to your class notes while reading at home and bring the insights from your reading to your class discussions.

Journal Keeping

You may be assigned to keep a reading journal for your class. Of course, you should follow your instructor's guidelines, but if you aren't sure what to write in a reading journal, think of it as a place to go a step further than you do in your annotations and notes. Try out possible answers, preferably several different ones, to the questions you have raised. Expand your ideas from single phrases and sentences into entire paragraphs, and see how they hold up under this deeper probing. Although a reading journal is substantially different from a personal journal or diary, it can at times contain reflections on any connections you make between a piece of literature and your own life and ideas. Some instructors ask students to respond to their readings with Web resources, including discussion boards, e-mail messages, or blog entries. These platforms allow you to build an archive of your responses so that you can easily return to them when you generate your paper draft; in addition, you can respond to other students as they develop their ideas. Here is an example of a Blackboard discussion board response to "Kubla Khan":

Forum: Kubla Khan
Date: Mon Jul 23 2007 22:15
Author: Diaz, Joanne
Subject: Under a spell?

I found it interesting that "Kubla Khan" didn't maintain a consistent meter or form. The poem begins in iambic tetrameter, with four pulses in each line, but as the poem gathers speed, it's as if that meter can't hold everything that the speaker wants to recount about his vision. Coleridge shifts to pentameter just as he begins to describe the "sinuous rills" (l. 8), then he expands his lines again in ll. 12-18. In that space, the poem's tempo gallops ahead, as if the speaker were out of breath. There are four sentences that end with exclamation points, which seem to elevate the excitement, and then the poem pulls back to pentameter again with the appearance of the strange fountain, and back again to tetrameter toward the end of the poem. In class, we discussed Coleridge's drug use and its effects on his writing process. I wonder, though, if the poem is trying to get at the difficulty of representing wondrous things with words, whether those things are drug-induced fantasies or not.

In this brief response, the student explores a series of questions about form and meter in Coleridge's poem. She asks: How and why does Coleridge vary the shape, sound, and rhythm of "Kubla Khan"? What is the relationship between Coleridge's poetics and the meaning of the poem? Note that the student cites specific passages that help her think about this problem, and refers to class discussion to establish connections with her own reading experience. This kind of response will serve the student when it's time to generate a thesis for her paper on the subject. Even if your instructor doesn't require a journal for your class, many students find it a useful tool for getting more out of their reading, not to mention a wealth of material to draw from when they sit down to write a paper.

Using Reference Materials

Many students are reluctant to use the dictionary or encyclopedia while reading, thinking they should be able to figure out the meanings of words from their context and not wanting to interrupt their reading. But the simple truth is that not all words are definable from context alone, and you'll get much more out of your reading if you are willing to make the small effort involved in looking up unknown words. If you are reading John Donne's "A Valediction: Forbidding Mourning" and you don't know what the word *valediction* means, you obviously start at a big disadvantage. A quick look at a dictionary would tell you that a valediction is a speech given at a time of parting (like the one a *valedict*orian gives at a graduation ceremony). Armed with that simple piece of information, you begin your reading of Donne's poem already knowing that it is about leaving someone or something, and understanding the poem becomes much simpler. An encyclopedia like *Britannica Online* (an online subscription service available at most university libraries) can also be a useful tool. If, as you're reading Donne's poem, you want to read his biography, *Britannica Online* can provide biographical and cultural context for his life and work. Or, if you want to learn more about the meter of the poem, you could look up "tetrameter" to develop an understanding of its use, or "conceit" to understand his comparison of two souls to "stiff twin compasses." *Britannica Online* often provides a bibliography for further reading, so it can be a good place to start your research.

ASKING CRITICAL QUESTIONS OF LITERATURE

As mentioned, one important part of active, critical reading is asking questions. If you are reading well, your textual annotations and notes will probably be full of questions. Some of these might be simple inquiries of fact, the sort of thing that can be answered by asking your instructor or by doing some quick research. But ideally, many of your questions will be more complex and meaty than that, the sort of probing queries that may have multiple, complex, or even contradictory answers. These are the questions that will provoke you and your classmates to think still more critically about the literature you read. You need not worry—at least not at first—about finding answers to all of your questions. As you work more with the text, discussing it with your instructor and classmates, writing about it, and reading other related stories, poems, and plays, you will begin to respond to the most important of the issues you've raised. And even if you never form a satisfactory answer to some questions, they will have served their purpose if they have made you think.

Questions about literature fall into one of four categories—those about the text, the author, the reader, and the cultural contexts of the work. Queries regarding the text can sometimes, though not always, be answered with a deeper examination of the story, poem, or play at hand.

Questions about the Text

Questions about a text are those that focus on issues such as **genre**, **structure**, language, and **style**. You might ask about the presence of certain images—or about their absence, if you have reason to expect them and find that they are not there. Sometimes authors juxtapose images or language in startling or unexpected ways, and you might ask about the purpose and effect of such **juxtaposition**. You might wonder about the meanings of specific words in the context of the work. (This is especially true with older works of literature, as meanings evolve and change over time, and a word you know today might have had a very different definition in the past.) When looking at a poem, you might inquire about the purpose and effect of sound, rhythm, rhyme, and so forth.

Your previous experiences are a big help here, including both your experiences of reading literature and your experiences in everyday life. You know from personal experience how you expect people to think and act in certain situations, and you can compare these expectations to the literature. What might motivate the characters or persons to think and act as they do? Your previous reading has likewise set up expectations for you. How does the text fulfill or frustrate these expectations? What other literature does this remind you of? What images seem arresting or unexpected? Where do the words seem particularly powerful, strange, or otherwise noteworthy?

Notice some of the questions one reader asked in his annotations upon first reading Ben Jonson's "On My First Son."

BEN JONSON   [1572–1637]

On My First Son

Farewell, thou child of my right hand, and joy;
My sin was too much hope of thee, loved boy:
Seven years thou' wert lent to me, and I thee pay,
Exacted by thy fate, on the just day.
O could I lose all father now! for why
Will man lament the state he should envy,
To have so soon 'scaped world's and flesh's rage,
And, if no other misery, yet age?
Rest in soft peace, and asked, say, "Here doth lie
Ben Jonson his best piece of poetry."
For whose sake henceforth all his vows be such
As what he loves may never like too much.

Why is hope for his child a "sin"?

The rhyme in ll. 1-2 aligns "joy" with "boy."

Why does the speaker treat the son like a bank transaction?

5

The word just has two meanings: exact and fair. Which does the poet mean?

What does he mean by this line? (confusing)

10

Here the poem works as a kind of epitaph on a tombstone.

Questions about the Author

When thinking about the connection between authors and the works they produce, two contradictory impulses come into play. One is the desire to ignore the biography of the author entirely and focus solely on the work at hand, and the other is to look closely at an author's life to see what might have led him or her to write a particular poem, story, or play. It is easy to understand the first impulse. After all, we are not likely to be able to ask an author what is meant by a certain line in a play or whether an image in a story is supposed to be read symbolically. The work of literature is what we have before us, and it should stand or fall on its own merits. This was, in fact, one of the principal tenets of **New Criticism**, a method of interpretation which dominated literary criticism for much of the twentieth century.

We cannot deny, however, that a writer's life does affect that writer's expression. An author's age, gender, religious beliefs, family structure, and many other factors have an impact on everything from topic choice to word choice. It is, therefore, appropriate sometimes to ask questions about an author as we try to come to a better understanding of a piece of literature. It is crucial, however, that we remember that not everything an author writes is to be taken at surface value. If, for instance, the narrator or principal character of a story is beaten or neglected by his parents, we should not jump to the conclusion that the author was an abused child. And if this character then goes on to justify his own actions by pointing to the abuse, we should also not assume that the author endorses this justification. In other words we must distinguish between narrative voice and the actual author as well as between what is written and what is meant.

This separation of biography and narrative is relatively easy to effect with stories and plays that we know to be fiction; just because a character says something doesn't necessarily mean the author believes it. Poetry is a little trickier though because it has the reputation of being straight from the heart. Not all poetry, however, is an accurate representation of its author's thoughts or beliefs. To give just two examples, T. S. Eliot's "The Love Song of J. Alfred Prufrock" voices the thoughts of the fictional Prufrock, not of Eliot himself, and many of the poems of Robert Browning are "dramatic monologues," delivered by speakers very different from Browning himself, including murderous noblemen and corrupt clergy.

Questions about the Cultural Context

We are all creatures of a particular time and place, and nobody, no matter how unique and iconoclastic, is immune to the subtle and pervasive force of social history. Many appropriate questions about literature, then, involve the cultural context of the work. What was going on in history at the time a piece of literature was written? Were there wars or other forms of social disruption? What was the standard of living for most people in the author's society? What was day-to-day life like? What were the typical religious beliefs and traditions? How was society organized in terms of power relations, work expectations, and educational possibilities? How about typical family structure? Did extended families live together? What were the expected gender roles inside (and outside) the family? All of these issues, and many more besides, have an impact on how authors see the world and how they respond to it in their writing.

As you read and ask questions of literature, you have another cultural context to be concerned with: your own. How does being a resident of twenty-first-century America affect your reading and understanding? We are every bit as influenced by issues of history, culture, and lifestyle as were authors and readers of the past, but it is harder for us to see this, since the dominant way of living tends to seem "natural" or even "universal." Indeed, one of the great benefits of reading literature is that it teaches us about history and helps us to understand and appreciate diverse cultures, not the least of which is our own.

In asking and answering the following questions about Ben Jonson's culture (seventeenth-century England), an attentive reader of "On My First Son" will also note features of our own present-day society, in which childhood death is relatively rare, family roles may be different, and religious attitudes and beliefs are considerably more diverse.

- How common was childhood death in the seventeenth century? What was the life expectancy?
- Typically, how involved were fathers in young children's lives at the time?
- Is the quotation in the poem (lines 9–10) the boy's epitaph?
- How difficult was life then? What exactly does Jonson mean by the "world's and flesh's rage"?
- How common was poetry on this topic? How "original" was Jonson's poem?
- What attitudes about God and heaven were common then? What was the conception of sin?

Questions about the Reader

Except in the case of private diaries, all writing is intended to be read by somebody, and an intended audience can have a big influence on the composition of the writing in question. Think about the differences in tone and structure between an e-mail you send to a friend and a paper you write for a course, and you'll get some idea of the impact of intended audience on a piece of writing. It is therefore worth considering a work's originally intended readers as you seek to understand a piece more fully. Who were these intended readers? Were they actually the people who read the literature when it was first published? How are readers' expectations fulfilled or disappointed by the structure and content of the literature? How did the original readers react? Was the work widely popular, or did only certain readers enjoy it? Did it have detractors as well? Was there any controversy over the work?

Of course, in addition to the original readers of any work of literature, there are also contemporary readers, including yourself. It is often said that great literature stands the test of time and can cross cultures to speak to many different sorts of people, but your reaction to a work may be very different from that of its original audience, especially if you are far removed from the work by time or culture. In earlier centuries in Europe and America, nearly all educated people were very familiar with the Bible and with stories and myths from Greek and Roman antiquity. Writers, therefore, could assume such knowledge on the part of their readers and make liberal reference in their work to stories and characters from these sources. Today many readers are less familiar with these sources, and we often need the help of footnotes or other study aids to understand such references. So what might have been enjoyable and enlightening for the original readers of a work might sometimes be tedious or frustrating for later readers. If we are to read a work critically, we must keep both past and present audiences in mind.

The first three questions following deal with the original audience of "On My First Son," while the final two compare this audience and a contemporary one.

- If childhood death was common in the seventeenth century, how would Jonson's readers have related to the subject of his poem?
- Did Jonson write this for wide circulation, or was it meant just for family and friends?
- Where was it first published, and who was likely to read it?
- Do readers with children of their own read it differently? Would I?
- Now that childhood death is fairly uncommon, do we take this poem more seriously than past readers? Or less seriously?

Looking over these questions about Jonson's poem — about the text, the author, the cultural context, and the reader — you will note that there are many differences among them. Some can be answered with a simple yes or no (*Is the quotation the boy's epitaph?*), while others require much more complex responses (*What was the conception of sin in Jonson's time?*). Others are matters of conjecture, opinion, or interpretation (*Do contemporary readers take this poem more seriously?*). Some can be answered simply by rereading and considering (*How can a child's death ever be considered fair?*), while others require discussion (*Do readers with children respond to the poem differently?*) or research (*Where was the poem first published?*).

Some inquiries you may have tentative answers for, as did the reader who asked these questions when she proposed both God and fate as potential candidates for who "lent" the child to the father. Others you won't be able to answer at first. If you are genuinely curious about any of them, do a little informal research to begin formulating answers. Some basic information can be found in the brief biographies or notes about authors that appear in most textbooks. There you could learn, for instance, the dates of Jonson's birth and death and some basic facts about his life and family. A quick look at a reputable reference work or Web site could provide still more valuable background information, like the fact that Jonson also lost his first daughter and that he wrote a poem about her death as well.

Having simply formulated some questions, you've already gone a long way toward understanding and interpreting a poem. If you bring such a list of questions with you to class, you will be more than ready to contribute to any discussion of the poem, and when the time comes to write an essay, you will find you have a rich mine of source material from which to draw.

TIPS FOR GOOD READING

A checklist of questions to ask yourself as you read and think about literary texts

☐ Have you *slowed down* and *reread* complex passages several times?

☐ Are you *looking up difficult words* in the dictionary to see if they have secondary meanings?

☐ Are you *annotating* the text by *underlining* key phrases? Writing questions or concerns in the *margins*?

☐ Are you taking your reading to the next level by asking *how* or *why* these passages are compelling to you?

☐ Are you marking those places in the text that make you feel uncomfortable, or present a worldview that feels strange to you?

☐ After you read, are you *taking notes* so that you can keep track of your ideas?

☐ Have you identified the **genre** of the text? Have you described its **style** and **tone**?

☐ Have you checked *Britannica Online* to learn more about the author and his or her **cultural context**?

☐ Have you reflected on your perspective as a twenty-first-century *reader*, and how that might affect your interpretation of literature from another time period?

CHAPTER 2

The Writing Process

CHOOSING A TOPIC

Obviously, your choice of a topic for your paper is of key importance, since everything else follows from that first decision. Your instructor may assign a specific topic or the choice may be left to you. The most important piece of advice we can give for choosing a topic is to write about something that genuinely interests you. If your instructor gives your class a choice, chances are he or she really wants to see a variety of topics and approaches and expects you to find a topic that works for *you*. You'll write a better paper if your topic is something of genuine interest to you. A bored or uncertain writer usually writes a boring or unconvincing paper. On the other hand, if you care about your topic, your enthusiasm will show in the writing, and the paper will be far more successful.

Even if your instructor assigns a fairly specific topic, you still need to spend a little time thinking about and working with it. You want your paper to stand out from the rest, and you should do whatever you can to make the assignment your own. When you receive an assignment, give some thought as to how it might relate to your own interests and how you might call upon your background and knowledge to approach the topic in fresh and interesting ways.

Finally, if you've put in some thought and effort but still don't know what to write about, remember that you do not need to go it alone. Seek out guidance and help. Talk with other students in your class and see what they have decided to write about; though of course you don't want simply to copy someone else's topic, hearing what others think can often spark a fresh idea. And don't forget your instructor. Most teachers are more than happy to spend a little time helping you come up with a topic and approach that will help you write a good paper.

DEVELOPING AN ARGUMENT

With the possible exception of a *summary* (a brief recap of a text's most important points), all writing about literature is to some degree a form of argument. Before proceeding, though, let's dispel some of the negative connotations of the word *argument*. In everyday usage, this term can connote a heated verbal fight, and it suggests two (or more) people growing angry and, often, becoming less articulate and more abusive as time passes. It suggests combat and implies that the other party in the process is an opponent. In this sort of argument, there are winners and losers.

Clearly this is not what we have in mind when we say you will be writing argumentatively about literature. Used in a different, more traditional sense, argument refers to a writer's or speaker's attempt to establish the validity of a given position. In other words, when you write a paper you work to convince your reader that what you are saying is valid and persuasive. The reader is not the enemy, not someone whose ideas are to be crushed and refuted, but rather a person whose thoughts and feelings you have a chance to affect. You are not arguing *against* your reader; rather, you are using your argumentative abilities to *help* your reader see the logic and value of your position.

The Thesis

To begin writing a literary argument, then, you must take a position and have a point to make. This principal point will be the *thesis* of your paper. It is important to distinguish between a topic and a thesis: Your topic is the issue or area upon which you will focus your attention, and your thesis is a statement *about* this topic.

Here is an example of a topic for Ben Jonson's "On My First Son" from a student journal:

Topic:

I am interested in the exploration of sin in Jonson's "On My First Son."

Here is an example of a thesis statement for Jonson's poem:

Thesis:

In "On My First Son," the speaker seems to use the death of his young son as a way to explore his own sin. However, the poet is just as interested in demonstrating his poetic mastery by drawing from an ancient Roman epigram as his model.

It might help to phrase your thesis as a complete sentence in which the topic is the subject, followed by a verb that makes a firm statement or claim regarding your topic. This is your **thesis statement**, and it will probably appear toward the beginning of your paper. The foremost purpose of a paper, then, is to explain, defend, and ultimately prove the truth of its thesis.

Keep the following guidelines in mind as you think about a tentative thesis for your paper.

- **Your thesis should be both clear and specific.** The purpose of a thesis is to serve as a guide to both the reader and the writer, so it needs to be understandable and to point clearly to the specific aspects of the literature that you will discuss. This does not mean it will stand alone or need no further development or explanation— after all that's what the rest of the paper is for. But a reader who is familiar with the story, poem, or play you are writing about (and it is fair to assume a basic familiarity) should have a good sense of what your thesis means and how it relates to the literature.

- **Your thesis should be relevant.** The claim you make should not only interest you as a writer but also give your reader a reason to keep reading by sparking his or her interest and desire to know more. Not every paper is going to change lives or minds, of course, but you should at least state your thesis in such a way that your reader won't have the most dreaded of responses: "Who cares?"

- **Your thesis should be debatable.** Since the purpose of an argumentative paper is to convince a reader that your thesis is correct (or at least that it has merit), it cannot simply be an irrefutable fact. A good thesis will be something that a reasonable person, having read the literature, might disagree with or might not have considered at all. It should give you something to prove.

- **Your thesis should be original.** Again, originality does not imply that every thesis you write must be a brilliant gem that nobody but you could have discovered. But it should be something you have thought about independently, it should avoid clichés, contain something of you, and do more than parrot back something said in your class or written in your textbook.

- **You should be able to state your thesis as a complete sentence.** This sentence, generally referred to as the *thesis statement*, should first identify your topic and then make a claim about it. (Occasionally, especially for longer papers with more complex ideas behind them, you will need more than one sentence to state your thesis clearly. Even in these cases, though, the complete thesis must both identify the topic and make a claim about it.)

- **Your thesis should be appropriate to the assignment.** This may seem obvious, but as we work with literature, taking notes, asking questions, and beginning to think about topics and theses, it is possible to lose sight of the assignment as it was presented. After you have come up with a tentative thesis, it's a good idea to go back and review the assignment as your instructor gave it, making sure your paper will fulfill its requirements.

You will note that in this discussion the phrase *tentative thesis* has come up a number of times. The word *tentative* is important. As you start to gather support and to write your paper, your thesis will help you focus clearly on your task and sort out which of your ideas, observations, and questions are relevant to the project at hand. But you should keep an open mind as well, realizing that your thesis is likely to evolve as you write. You are likely to change the focus in subtle or not so subtle ways, and it's even possible that you will change your mind completely as you write and therefore need to create a new thesis from scratch. If this happens, don't regard it as a failure. On the contrary, it means you have succeeded in learning something genuine from the experience of writing, and that is what a literature class is all about.

GATHERING SUPPORT FOR YOUR THESIS

Once you have crafted a tentative thesis, it is time to think about the evidence or support you will need to convince your reader of the claim's validity. But what exactly counts as support? What can you include in your paper as evidence that your thesis is true? Essentially, all support comes from one of three sources:

- **The text itself is the most obvious source of support.** It is not enough to *say* that a certain piece of literature says or means a certain thing. You will need to *show* this by summarizing, paraphrasing, or quoting the literature itself.
- **Other people's ideas are a good source of support.** Chances are you will find a lot of useful material for your paper if you pay attention to easily available sources of ideas from other readers. These include the notes and biographical information in your textbooks, research conducted online or in the library, lectures and discussions in class, and even informal conversations about the literature with your friends and classmates.
- **Your own thoughts are your most important source of support.** Remember that although you may want to integrate ideas and

information from a variety of sources, your paper is yours and as such should reflect *your* thinking. The most indispensable source of material for your paper is your own mind; your own thoughts and words should always carry the heaviest weight in any paper you write.

Organizing Your Paper

Once you've determined what evidence to use, it is time to begin sorting and organizing it. The organizing principle for any paper is the sequence of paragraphs, so at this stage you should be thinking at the level of paragraph content. Remember that each paragraph should contain one main idea and sufficient evidence and explanation to support that idea. When added together, these paragraph-level ideas lead a reader to your paper's ultimate point—your thesis. So the first stage of organizing the content of your essay is to cluster together similar ideas in order to begin shaping the substance of individual paragraphs. The second stage is to determine the order in which these paragraphs will appear.

As you write and revise your paper, you may have different ideas about how to structure it. You may want to put the topic sentence somewhere other than at the beginning of a paragraph, or perhaps the topic is so clear that no specific topic sentence is even needed. You may devise a more interesting way to structure your introduction or conclusion. (Some additional, more specific thoughts for those tricky introductory and concluding paragraphs follow.) Unless your instructor has specified the form in which your paper is to be organized, you should feel free to experiment a bit. You may end up using some parts of the structure described above while rejecting others. Look, for instance, at this introduction to a research paper on Emily Dickinson:

> With a keen eye for detail and a steadfast "resilience not to be overcome by mysteries that eluded religion, science, and the law" (Eberwein 42), Emily Dickinson's poetry records the abstractions of human life so matter-of-factly that her readers often take her technical skill for granted. Take, for example, the six-stanza poem "Because I could not stop for Death"—a detached, but never completely dispassionate, recollection of a human's journey to its final conclusion. The verse is crafted so succinctly and with such precision that its complex and vivid images are made even more extraordinary and meaningful. We might expect literature on the theme of death to invoke religious imagery,

stillness, and a sense of dread or foreboding, but none of this is the case. Instead, the poem challenges the preconceptions Dickinson's contemporaries had about death, and in doing so it makes us challenge ours as well.

In this introduction, this student sets up a common idea about Dickinson's poetry (that it's written in a matter-of-fact style) and suggests that Dickinson's compression actually reveals literary complexity, and a challenge to contemporary attitudes about death. Notice, too, that the student engages with literary criticism to set up his claims about Dickinson's work. He begins not with a sweeping generalization or a philosophical statement but rather with a specific observation and a quotation about Emily Dickinson's beliefs and styles. He does, however, conclude the opening paragraph with a thesis statement suggesting to readers the content, scope, and argument of his paper.

For most writers, creating some version of an outline is the best way to approach the task of organizing evidence into a logical sequence for a paper. In the past you may have been asked to write a formal outline, complete with Roman numerals and capital letters. If this technique has been helpful in organizing your thoughts, by all means continue to use it. For many writers, however, an informal outline works just as well and is less cumbersome. To construct an informal outline, simply jot down a heading that summarizes the topic of each paragraph you intend to write. Then cluster your gathered evidence — quotations or paraphrases from the literature, ideas for analysis, and so on — into groups under the headings.

The following is an example of an informal outline for a paper on Shakespeare's Sonnet 116. In this outline, the student focuses on the positive and negative language in the poem and how it results in a more interesting definition of love than he had seen in other love poems.

Introduction
    Two kinds of typical love poems: happy and sad
    Sonnet 116 is more complex and interesting
    <u>Tentative thesis</u>: By including both negative and positive
        images and language, this sonnet gives a complex and
        realistic definition of love.

Vivid images in poem
    <u>Positive/expected</u>: "star," "ever-fixèd mark," "rosy lips and cheeks"

> Negative/unexpected: "sickle" (deathlike), "wandering bark" (lost
>   boat), "tempests"

Negative language
> words/phrases: "Let me not," "Love is not," "never," "nor," "no," etc.
> abstractions: "alteration," "impediments," "error"

Conclusion
> Love never changes
> Shakespeare's definition still works some 400 years later

This is not, obviously, a formal outline. It does, however, group similar items and ideas together, and it gives the writer a basic structure to follow as he continues with the composing process.

DRAFTING, REVISING, AND EDITING

You have a topic. You have a tentative thesis. You have gathered evidence. You have an outline or tentative structure in mind for this evidence. It is time to begin writing your first draft. Every writer has his or her own slightly different process for getting the words down on paper. Some begin at the beginning of the paper, or with the first body paragraph, and work straight through to the end in a clear, organized fashion. Others write bits and pieces of the paper out of order and allow the overall structure to emerge at a later time.

Some writers claim that they work better at the last minute and focus better under the pressure of a looming deadline. This, however, is almost always a justification for sloppy work habits, and procrastination rarely if ever really results in a superior paper. When habitual procrastinators change their working methods and give themselves more time on a project, they are frequently surprised to discover that the process is more enjoyable and the final product of their efforts better than what they have produced in the past. Start early and work steadily—it will prove more than worth it.

The process of writing breaks down roughly into prewriting, drafting, revising, and finally, editing and proofreading. Prewriting includes everything that you need to do before you draft your essay, including brainstorming, choosing a topic, developing a tentative thesis, and considering possible support.

- **Brainstorming.** You can brainstorm—alone or with classmates—to explore the many possible threads that you could follow in your writing. Don't censor yourself during this process. Allow yourself to write down everything that interests, puzzles, or delights you.
- **Choosing a topic.** Once you're done with your brainstorming, it's time to choose one topic out of the many that you've explored. Is there a recurring theme that interests you? A juxtaposition that provides a rich complexity? A cultural context that bears on your understanding of the text?
- **Developing a tentative thesis.** In this prewriting stage, keep your thesis flexible. When you're done with your first draft, you can always go back to change your thesis so that it better matches what you've discovered in the writing process.
- **Considering possible support.** At this stage, use every resource available to you to find support for your thesis. What lines in the poem, short story, or play reinforce your claims? Have you looked up words in the dictionary? Have you checked difficult concepts in a respectable encyclopedia or other reference? Have you asked your teacher for further reading suggestions? Have you read articles or book chapters that are appropriate to your topic, and are you formulating your responses to them?

Drafting

Try to write your first draft fairly quickly. You don't need to get every sentence just right—that's what the revision phase of writing is for. What you want now is just to get as much good raw material as possible into the mix and see what works. Don't worry too much yet about style, transitions, grammar, and so forth. In fact, you don't even need to start at the beginning or work right through to the end. If you get stuck on one part, move on. You can always come back and fill in the gaps later. Introductions can be especially tricky, particularly since you haven't yet finished the essay and don't really know what it is you're introducing. Some writers find it easier to just start with the body of the essay, or to write a short, sloppy introduction as a placeholder. You can go back and work on the real introduction when the draft is complete.

Revising

Once you have a complete, or near complete, draft, it's time to begin thinking about revision. Try to avoid the common pitfall of thinking of revision as locating and fixing mistakes. Revision is far more than this. Looking at the parts of the word, you can see that *re-vision* means seeing again, and indeed the revision stage of the writing process is your chance to see your draft anew and make real and substantial improvements to every facet of it, from its organization to its tone to your word choices. Most successful writers will tell you that it is in the revision stage that the real work gets done, where the writing takes shape and begins to emerge in its final form. Don't skimp on this part of the process or try to race through it.

It is a good idea not to start a major revision the minute a draft is complete. Take a break. Exercise, have a meal, do something completely different to clear your mind. If possible, put the draft aside for at least a day so that when you return to it you'll have a fresh perspective and can begin truly re-seeing it. Print out your draft. Attempting serious revision on-screen is generally a bad idea—we see differently, and we usually see more, when we read off a printed page. Read with a pen in your hand and annotate your text just the way you would a piece of literature, looking for the strengths and weaknesses of your argument. We suggest a three-phase process, consisting of **global revisions**, or large-scale revisions; **local revisions**, or small-scale revisions; and a final **editing and proofreading**. If you haven't done so before, revising your paper three times may seem like a lot of work, but bear in mind that most professional writers revise their work many more times than that, and revision is the real key to writing the best paper you can.

Global Revision

On a first pass at revision—the large-scale, global part of the process—don't worry too much about details like word choice, punctuation, and so forth. Too many students focus so much on these issues that they miss the big picture. The details are important, but you will deal with them in depth later. You wouldn't want to spend your time getting the wording of a sentence just right only to decide later that the paragraph it is in weakens your argument and needs to be deleted. So at first, look at the overall picture—the argument, organization, and tone of the paper as a whole. While there's nothing wrong with making a few small improvements as you read, nothing smaller than a paragraph should concern you at this point. Here are some possibilities for how you might revise your paper globally.

TIPS FOR DRAFTING, REVISING, AND EDITING

Further develop your focus and thesis.

☐ Can your reader immediately identify what the topic of the essay will be—that is, which text(s) you will analyze, and which angle of the text (for example, the use of one word or phrase in one or two poems)?

☐ Have you narrowed the scope of the thesis for your reader? How could it be further narrowed? Remember, it's not enough to say "Women are portrayed differently in X and Y." What do you mean by "differently"? Get as specific as possible.

☐ Does your thesis clearly identify a claim that is contestable but valid?

☐ Has your thinking about the issues evolved as you have written? If so, how will you change the thesis statement?

☐ Have you answered the larger "So what?" question? This is the question that the thesis should attempt to answer. Of course, the thesis is not entirely responsible for this; however, this is the place to get your reader thinking about why this argument is important.

Reorganize your paper, if necessary.

☐ Does the order of the ideas and paragraphs make immediate sense to you, or does some alternate structure suggest itself?

Expand your paper with new paragraphs or with new evidence within existing paragraphs.

☐ What textual evidence have you used? Is it sufficiently provocative and persuasive? Or does it veer off into another direction?

☐ Have you successfully integrated quotations into your own writing, while at the same time acknowledging your source? A quotation that is unintroduced or uncontextualized, left disconnected from your sentences, is a good sign that you haven't thought enough about how this textual evidence supports your larger point—how it fits into your framework.

Eliminate any unnecessary, contradictory, or distracting passages.

☐ Does every piece of evidence, every sentence, and every paragraph contribute to the validity of your argument? If not, eliminate extraneous discussions and save them for another project.

Clarify difficult passages with more specific explanations or evidence.

☐ Have you worked to convey why you are citing a particular passage? What *particular* details in it provide evidence that supports your interpretation? You can assume that your reader has read your text, but cannot assume that they interpret it in the same way you do.

Once you have completed your first, large-scale revision, chances are you will feel more confident about the content and structure of your paper. The thesis and focus are strong, the evidence is lined up, the major points are clear. Print out the new version, take another break if you can, and prepare to move on to the second phase of revision, the one that takes place at the local level of words, phrases, and sentences.

Local Revision

The focus here is on style and clarity. The types of changes you will make in this stage are, essentially, small-scale versions of the changes you made in the first round of revision: adding, cutting, reorganizing, and clarifying. Are you sure about the meanings of any difficult or unusual words you have used? Is there enough variety in sentence style to keep your writing interesting? Do the same words or phrases appear again and again? Are the images vivid? Are the verbs strong? One way to assess the effectiveness of a paper's style is to read it aloud and hear how it sounds. You may feel a little foolish doing this, but many people find it very helpful.

Final Editing and Proofreading

Once you have revised your essay a second time and achieved both content and a style that pleases you, it's time for **final editing**. This is where you make it "correct."

FINAL EDITING CHECKLIST

Spelling

☐ Have you spelled everything correctly? (Should it be *their* or *there*? *It's* or *its*?)

Punctuation

☐ Look for things that have caused you trouble in the past. Should you use a comma or a semicolon? Does the period go inside or outside of the quotation marks?

Formatting

☐ Have you italicized or underlined titles of plays and novels (*Othello* or *The Woman Warrior*), and put the titles of short stories and poems in quotation marks ("Love in L.A.," "The Fish")?

☐ Have you put quoted excerpts from the text in quotation marks?

☐ Does your Works Cited list follow MLA format, and do you properly cite your quotations in the body of the text? Nobody expects you to know all the rules on your own, but you should know where to look for them. If you have questions about citation and formatting, look them up in this book or in a good dictionary, grammar handbook, or other reference. A good online source is Diana Hacker's *Research and Documentation Online*: http://www.dianahacker.com/resdoc/.

Here is a paragraph from a student essay on *Hamlet*. Notice the kinds of corrections that the student will have to make before the paragraph is done.

The supernatural relm affects the revenge tragedy in other ways than the appearance and presence of ghosts. In Hamlet, the religious concern with final absolution both inflames Hamlet's desire for revenge and also causes him to hesitate in carrying out revenge. Not only has Hamlet's father been murdered, but he was also Cut off even in the blossoms of [his] sin, / Unhousled,

Spelling: "realm"

Italicize "Hamlet."

disappointed, unanel'd, / No reck'ning made, but sent to [his] account / With all [his] imperfections on [his] head (1. 5. 77–80). For Hamlet's father, being murdered is doubly disastrous; not only is his life cut short. But he must burn away "the foul crimes done in [his] days of nature" in purgatory before he can be granted access to heaven (1. 5. 13). A normal death would have afforded him final absolution, and thus a direct route to heaven. The same concern that makes Hamlet's father's death even more terrible also causes Hamlet to pass on a perfect opportunity to exact revenge on his father's murderer. Hamlet finds Claudius praying, alone. To kill a man in prayer means to kill a man who has had all his sins absolved. Hamlet observes Claudius and reasons: "A villain kills my father, and for that, / I, his sole son, do this same villain send / To heaven." (3. 3. 76–8) Hamlet's concern for the supernatural afterlife affects his carrying out revenge.

Remember to [...] quotation m[...] around the d[...] quotation.

This should [...] comma joini[...] two sentence[...] fragments.

This period [...] belongs ou[...] the parenth[...] after the ac[...] scene, and [...] number.

PEER EDITING AND WORKSHOPS

One final word of advice as you revise your paper: Ask for help. Doing so is neither cheating nor is it an admission of defeat. In fact, professional writers do it all the time. Despite the persistent image of writers toiling in isolation, most successful writers seek advice at various stages. More important, they are willing to listen to that advice and to rethink what they have written if it seems not to be communicating what they had intended.

Some instructors give class time for draft workshops, sometimes called peer editing, in which you work with your fellow students, trying to help one another improve your work-in-progress. Such workshops can benefit you in two ways. First, your classmates can offer you critiques and advice on what you might have missed in your own rereading. Second, reading and discussing papers other than your own will help you to grow as a writer, showing you a variety of ways in which a topic can be approached. If you really like something about a peer's paper—say, a vivid introduction or the effective use of humor—make note of how it works within the paper and consider integrating something similar into a future paper of your own. We are not, of course, advocating copying your classmates; rather, we are pointing out that other people's writing has much to teach us.

Some students are uncomfortable with such workshops. They may feel they don't know enough about writing to give valid advice to others, or they may doubt whether advice from their peers is particularly valuable. But you don't need to be a great literary critic, much less an expert on style or grammar, in order to give genuinely useful advice to a fellow writer. Whatever your skills or limitations as a writer, you have something invaluable to give: the thoughts and impressions of a real reader working through a paper. It is only when we see how a reader responds to what we've written that we know if a paper is communicating its intended message. If you are given an opportunity to engage in peer workshops, make the most of them.

Your instructor may give you guidelines regarding what to look for in others' drafts, or you may be left more or less on your own. In either case, keep these general guidelines in mind.

- **Be respectful of one another's work.** You should, of course, treat your peers' work with the same respect and seriousness that you'd want for your own. Keep your criticism constructive and avoid personal attacks, even if you disagree strongly with an opinion. You can help your fellow writers by expressing a contrary opinion in a civilized and thoughtful manner.

- **Be honest.** This means giving real, constructive criticism when it is due. Don't try to spare your workshop partner's feelings by saying "That's great" or "It's fine," when it really isn't. When asked what went badly in a peer workshop, students most commonly respond *not* that their peers were too harsh on their work but that they were not harsh enough. Wouldn't you rather hear about a problem with your work from a peer in a draft workshop than from your professor after you have already handed in the final draft? So would your classmates.

- **Look for the good as well as the bad in a draft.** No paper, no matter how rough or problematic, is completely without merit. And no paper, no matter how clever or well written, couldn't be improved. By pointing out both what works and what doesn't, you will help your classmates grow as writers.

- **Keep an eye on the time.** It's easy to get wrapped up in a discussion of an interesting paper and not allow adequate time to another. Say you're given half an hour to work with your draft and that of one classmate. When you reach the fifteen-minute mark, move on, no matter how interesting your discussion is. Fair is fair. On the other hand, don't stop short of the allotted time. If you are really reading carefully and thinking hard about one another's drafts, it should be impossible to finish early.

- **Take notes, on your draft itself or on a separate sheet.** You may be certain that you will remember what was said in a workshop, but you would be amazed how often people forget the good advice they heard and intended to follow. Better safe than sorry—take careful notes.

- **Ask questions.** Asking questions about portions of a draft you don't understand or find problematic can help its writer see what needs to be clarified, expanded, or reworked. Useful questions can range from the large scale (*What is the purpose of this paragraph?*) to the small (*Is this a quote? Who said it?*).

- **Don't assume that explaining yourself to your workshop partner can replace revision.** Sometimes your workshop partners will ask a question, and when you answer it for them they will say, "Oh, right, that makes sense," leaving you with the impression that everything is clear now. But remember, your classmates didn't understand it from the writing alone and you won't be there to explain it to your teacher.

- **Be specific in your comments.** Vague comments like "The introduction is good" or "It's sort of confusing here" are not much help. Aim for something more like "The introduction was funny and really made me want to read on" or "This paragraph confused me because it seems to contradict what you said in the previous one." With comments like these, a writer will have a much better sense of where to focus his or her revision energies.

- **Try to focus on the big picture.** It's tempting when reading a draft to zero in on distracting little mistakes in spelling, punctuation, or word choice. While it's generally fine to point out or circle such surface matters as you go along, a draft workshop is not about correcting mistakes. It's about helping one another to re-see and rethink your papers on a global scale.

- **Push your partners to help you more.** If your workshop partners seem shy or reluctant to criticize, prompt them to say more by letting them know that you really want advice and that you are able to take criticism. Point out to them what you perceive as the trouble spots in the essay, and ask if they have any ideas to help you out. It feels good, of course, to hear that someone likes your paper and cannot imagine how to improve it. But in the long run it is even better to get real, useful advice that will lead to a better paper. If your classmates are not helping you enough, it's your responsibility to ask for more.

Even if your class does not include workshop time, this in no way prevents you from using the many resources available to you on campus. Find one or two other members of your class and make time to have your own peer workshop, reading and critiquing one another's drafts. Be sure to arrange such a meeting far enough in advance of the due date so that you will have ample time to implement any good revision advice you receive. Many campuses also have writing or tutoring centers, and the workers in these centers, often advanced students who are skilled writers, can offer a good deal of help. Remember, again, that you should make an appointment to see a tutor well in advance of the paper's due date, and you should *not* expect a tutor to revise or "fix" your paper for you. That is, ultimately, your job. And, of course, you can also approach your instructor at any phase of the writing process and ask for advice and help.

But remember, no matter where you turn for advice, the final responsibility for your paper is yours. Any advice and help you receive from classmates, tutors, friends—or even your instructor—is just that: advice and help. It is *your* paper, and *you* must be the one to make the decisions about which advice to follow, which to ignore, and how to implement changes to improve your paper. The key is to keep an open mind, seek help from all available sources, and give yourself plenty of time to turn your first draft into a final paper that makes you truly proud.

TROUBLE SPOTS

Ideally, of course, your entire paper will be equally compelling and polished, but there are certain points in a paper that most often cause trouble for writers and readers, and these points may require a little additional attention on your part. The most typical trouble spots are introductory and concluding paragraphs and the transitional sentences that connect paragraphs. Although there is no one formula to help you to navigate these waters, as each writing situation and each paper is different, there are some general guidelines that can help you think through the problems that might arise in these areas.

Introductions

Essentially, an introduction accomplishes two things. First, it gives a sense of both your topic and your approach to that topic, which is why it is common to make your thesis statement a part of the introduction. Second, an introduction compels your readers' interest and makes them want to read on and find out what your paper has to say. Some common strategies used in effective introductions are to begin with a probing rhetorical question, a vivid description, or an intriguing quotation. Weak introductions tend to speak in generalities or in philosophical ideas that are only tangentially related to the real topic of your paper. Don't spin your wheels: get specific and get to the point right away.

Consider this introduction from a student essay on Susan Glaspell's *Trifles*:

> What is the relationship between legality and morality? Susan Glaspell's short play *Trifles* asks us to ponder this question, but it provides no clear answers. Part murder mystery, part battle of the sexes, the play makes its readers confront and question many issues about laws, morals, and human relationships. In the person of Mrs. Peters, a sheriff's wife, the play chronicles one woman's moral journey from a certain, unambiguous belief in the law to a more situational view of ethics. Before it is over, this once legally minded woman is even willing to cover up the truth and let someone get away with murder.

The student poses a philosophical question at the very beginning of the paper and then offers a tentative answer.

Conclusions

Your conclusion should give your reader something new to think about, a reason not to just forget your essay. Some writers like to use the conclusion to return to an idea, a quotation, or an image first raised in the introduction, creating a satisfying feeling of completeness and self-containment.

In this example from the same student paper, note how the student offers a tentative answer in her conclusion:

> In the end, Mrs. Peters gives in to what she believes to be emotionally right rather than what is legally permissible. She collaborates with Mrs. Hale to cover up evidence of the motive and hide the dead canary. Though very little time has gone by, she has undergone a major transformation. She may be, as the county attorney says, "married to the law," but she is also divorced from her old ideals. When she tries to cover up the evidence, a stage direction says she "goes to pieces," and Mrs. Hale has to help her. By the time she pulls herself together, the new

> woman she is will be a very different person from the old one. She, along
> with the reader, is now in a world where the relationship between legality
> and morality is far more complex than she had ever suspected.

Some writers use the conclusion to show the implications of their claims
or the connections between the literature and real life. This is your
chance to make a good final impression, so don't waste it with simple
summary and restatement.

Transitions

Each paragraph is built around a different idea, and the job of the transitions is to show how these separate ideas are related to one another, to
make the juxtaposition of two paragraphs seem as logical to a reader as
it is to the writer. When you fear a transition isn't working effectively, the
first question you should ask yourself is *why* does one paragraph follow
another in this particular order? Would it make more sense to change
the placement of some paragraphs, or is this really the best organizational strategy for this portion of the paper? Once you know why your
paper is structured as it is, transitions become much easier to write,
simply making apparent to your audience the connections you already
know to be there. As you begin each new paragraph, give some consideration to the links between it and the previous paragraph, and try to make
those links explicit in the opening sentence.

As with any other aspect of your writing, if you've had trouble in the
past with introductions, conclusions, or transitions, one of your best
sources of help is to be an attentive reader of others' writing. Pay special
attention to these potential trouble spots in the writing you admire,
whether by a classmate or a professional author, and see how he or she
navigates them. Don't stick with the writing methods that have caused
you headaches in the past. Be willing to try out different strategies, seeing which ones work best for you. In time you'll find you have a whole
array of ways to approach these trouble spots, and you'll be able to find
a successful response to each particular writing situation.

TIPS FOR WRITING ABOUT LITERATURE

Each genre of literature—fiction, poetry, and drama—poses its own,
slightly different set of assumptions and problems for writers, which are
covered in more detail in the sections that follow. However, there are certain general principles that can help you as you write about any form of
literature.

- **Don't assume that your readers will remember (or consider important) the same ideas or incidents in the literature that you do.** You should assume that your readers have *read* the literature but not necessarily that they have reacted to it the same way you have. Therefore, whenever possible, use specific examples and evidence in the form of quotations and summaries to back up your claims.
- **Do not retell the plot or text at length.** Some writers are tempted to begin with a plot summary or even to include the text of a short poem at the beginning of a paper. However, this strategy can backfire by delaying the real substance of your paper. Be discriminating when you summarize — keep quotations short and get to the *point* you want to make as quickly as possible.
- **Do not assume that quotations or summaries are self-sufficient and prove your point automatically.** Summaries and quotations are a starting point; you need to *analyze* them thoroughly in your own words, explaining why they are important. As a general rule, each quotation or summary should be followed by at least several sentences of analysis.
- **It is customary to use the present tense when writing about literature,** even if the events discussed take place in the distant past. Example:

When she sees that Romeo is dead, Juliet kills herself with his knife.

- **The first time you mention an author, use his or her full name.** For subsequent references, the last name is sufficient. (Do not use first names only; it sounds as if you know an author personally.)
- **Titles of poems, stories, and essays should be put in quotation marks. Titles of books, plays, and periodicals (magazines, newspapers, etc.) should be underlined or italicized.** In titles and in all quotations, follow spelling, capitalization, and punctuation *exactly* as it occurs in the work itself.
- **Give your paper a title.** A title doesn't need to be elaborate or super clever, but it should give some clue as to what the paper is about and begin setting up expectations for your reader. Simply restating the assignment, such as "Essay #2" or "Comparison and Contrast Paper," is of little help to a reader and might even suggest intellectual laziness on the part of the writer. For the same reason, avoid giving your paper the same title as the work of literature you are writing about; unless you're Shakespeare or Hemingway, don't title your paper *Hamlet* or "A Clean, Well-Lighted Place."
- **Above all, use common sense and *be consistent.***

USING QUOTATIONS EFFECTIVELY

At some point, you will want to quote the literature you are writing about, and you might also want to quote some secondary research sources as well. Be selective, though, in your use of **quotations** so that the dominant voice of the paper is your own, not a patchwork of the words of others. Here is general advice to help you integrate quotations effectively into your essays.

Try to avoid **floating quotations**. Sometimes writers simply lift a sentence out of the original, put quotation marks around it, and identify the source (if at all) in a subsequent sentence.

> "I met a traveler from an antique land." This is how Shelley's poem
> "Ozymandias" begins.

Doing so can create confusion for a reader, who is momentarily left to ponder where the quotation comes from and why have you quoted it. In addition to potentially causing confusion, such quoting can read as awkward and choppy, as there is no transition between another writer's words and yours.

Use at least an **attributed quotation**; that is, one that names the source *within* the sentence containing the quotation, usually in a lead-in phrase.

> Shelley begins his poem "Ozymandias" with the words, "I met a traveler
> from an antique land."

This way the reader knows right away who originally wrote or said the quoted material and knows (or at least expects) that your commentary will follow. It also provides a smoother transition between your words and the quotation.

Whenever possible, use an **integrated quotation**. To do this, you make the quotation a part of your own sentence.

> When the narrator of "Ozymandias" begins by saying that he "met a
> traveler from an antique land," we are immediately thrust into a
> mysterious world.

This is the hardest sort of quoting to do since it requires that you make the quoted material fit in grammatically with your own sentence, but the payoff in clarity and sharp prose is usually well worth the extra time spent on sentence revision.

Adding to or Altering a Quotation

Sometimes, especially when you are using integrated quotations effectively, you will find that you need to slightly alter the words you are
quoting. You should, of course, keep quotations exact whenever possible,
but occasionally the disparity between the tense, point of view, or grammar of your sentence and that of the quoted material will necessitate
some alterations. Other difficulties can arise when you quote a passage
that already contains a quotation or when you need to combine quotation marks with other punctuation marks. When any of these situations
arise, the following guidelines should prove useful. The examples of
quoted text that follow are all drawn from this original passage from
Hamlet, in which Hamlet and his friend Horatio are watching a
gravedigger unearth old skulls in a cemetery:

> HAMLET: That skull had a tongue in it, and could sing once. How the
> knave jowls it to the ground, as if 'twere Cain's jaw-bone, that did the
> first murder! This might be the pate of a politician, which this ass
> now o'erreaches, one that would circumvent God, might it not?
> HORATIO: It might, my lord.
> HAMLET: Or of a courtier, which could say "Good morrow, sweet lord!
> How dost thou, sweet lord?" This might be my Lord Such-a-one, that
> prais'd my Lord Such-a-one's horse when 'a meant to beg it, might
> it not?

If you ever alter anything in a quotation or add words to it in order to
make it clear and grammatically consistent with your own writing, you
need to signal to your readers what you have added or changed. This is
done by enclosing your words within square brackets in order to distinguish them from those in the source. If, for instance, you feel Hamlet's reference to the gravedigger as "this ass" is unclear, you could clarify it either
by substituting your own words, as in the first example here, or by adding
the identifying phrase to the original quote, as in the second example:

> Hamlet wonders if it is "the pate of a politician, which [the gravedigger]
> now o'erreaches."

> Hamlet wonders if it is "the pate of a politician, which this ass [the
> gravedigger] now o'erreaches."

Omitting Words from a Quotation

In order to keep a quotation focused and to the point, you will some
times want to omit words, phrases, or even whole sentences that do no
contribute to your point. Any omission is signaled by **ellipses**, or thre

spaced periods, with square brackets around them. (The brackets are required to distinguish your own ellipses from any that might occur in the original source.)

> Hamlet wonders if the skull "might be the pate of a politician [...] that would circumvent God."

It is usually not necessary to use ellipses at the beginning or end of a quotation, since a reader assumes you are quoting only a relevant portion of text.

Quotations within Quotations

If you are quoting material that itself contains a quotation, the internal quotation is set off with single quotation marks rather than the standard double quotation marks that will enclose the entire quotation.

> Hamlet wonders if he might be looking at the skull "of a courtier, which could say 'Good morrow, sweet lord! How dost thou, sweet lord?'"

When the text you're quoting contains *only* material already in quotation marks in the original, the standard double quotation marks are all you need.

> Hamlet wonders if the courtier once said "Good morrow, sweet lord! How dost thou, sweet lord?"

Quotation Marks with Other Punctuation

When a period or a comma comes at the end of a quotation, it should always be placed inside the closing quotation marks, whether or not this punctuation was in the original source. In the first example that follows, note that the period following "horse" is within the quotation marks, even though there is no period there in the original. In the second example, the comma following "once" is also within the quotation marks, even though in Shakespeare's original "once" is followed by a period.

> Hamlet muses that the skull might have belonged to "my Lord Such-a-one, that prais'd my Lord Such-a-one's horse."

> "That skull had a tongue in it, and could sing once," muses Hamlet.

Other marks of punctuation (semicolons, question marks, etc.), are placed inside quotation marks if they are part of the original quotation and outside of the marks if they are part of your own sentence but not of the passage you are quoting. In the first example, the question is Hamlet's, and so the question mark must be placed within the quotation marks; in the second example, the question is the essay writer's, and so the question mark is placed outside of the quotation marks.

> Hamlet asks Horatio if the skull "might be my Lord Such-a-one, that prais'd my Lord Such-a-one's horse when 'a meant to beg it, might it not?"

> Why is Hamlet so disturbed that this skull "might be the pate of a politician"?

These sorts of punctuation details are notoriously hard to remember, so you should not feel discouraged if you begin forgetting such highly specialized rules moments after reading them. At least know where you can look them up and do so when you proofread your paper. A willingness to attend to detail is what distinguishes serious students and gives writing a polished, professional appearance. Also, the more you work with quotations, the easier it will be to remember the rules.

Quoting from Stories

The guidelines that follow should be used not only when you quote from stories but also when you quote from any prose work, be it fiction or nonfiction.

Short Quotations

For short quotations of four lines or fewer, run the quotation in with your own text, using quotation marks to signal the beginning and end of the quotation.

> Young Goodman Brown notices that the branches touched by his companion "became strangely withered and dried up, as with a week's sunshine."

Long Quotations

When a quotation is longer than four lines in your text, set it off from your essay by beginning a new line and indenting it one inch from the left margin only, as shown here. This is called a block quotation:

Young Goodman Brown then notices something strange about his companion:

> As they went, he plucked a branch of maple to serve for a walking stick, and began to strip it of the twigs and little boughs, which were wet with evening dew. The moment his fingers touched them they became strangely withered and dried up, as with a week's sunshine.

Note that no quotation marks are used with block quotations. The indentation is sufficient to signal to your readers that this is a quotation.

Quoting from Poems

Short Quotations

For quotations of up to three lines, run the text right into your own, using quotation marks just as you would with a prose quotation. However, since the placement of line endings can be significant in a poem, you need to indicate where they occur. This is done by including a slash mark, with a single space on each side, where the line breaks occur. (Some students find this awkward looking at first, but you will quickly get used to it. Your instructor will expect you to honor the poet's choices regarding line breaks.)

> In "Sailing to Byzantium," Yeats describes an old man as "a paltry thing, / A tattered coat upon a stick."

Long Quotations

For quotations of four lines or more, "block" the material, setting it off one inch from the left margin, duplicating all line breaks of the original. Do not use quotation marks with block quotations.

> In "Sailing to Byzantium," Yeats describes both the ravages of age and the possibility of renewal in the poem's second stanza:
>
> > An aged man is but a paltry thing,
> > A tattered coat upon a stick, unless
> > Soul clap its hands and sing, and louder sing
> > For every tatter in its mortal dress,
> > Nor is there singing school but studying
> > Monuments of its own magnificence.

Quoting from Plays

Short Single-Speaker Passages

When you quote a short passage of drama with a single speaker, treat the quoted text just as you would prose fiction:

> Nora's first words in *A Doll House* are "Hide the tree well, Helene. The children mustn't get a glimpse of it till this evening, after it's trimmed."

Longer or More Complex Passages

For a longer quotation, or a quotation of any length involving more than one character, you will need to block off the quotation. Begin each separate piece of dialogue indented one inch from the left margin with the character's name, typed in all capital letters, followed by a period. Subsequent lines of the character's speech should be indented an additional quarter inch. (Your word processor's "hanging indent" function is useful for achieving this effect without having to indent each separate line.) As with fiction or poetry, do not use quotation marks for block quotations.

> We see the tension between Nora and her husband in their very first confrontation:
>
> NORA. Oh, but Torvald, this year we really should let
>   ourselves go a bit. It's the first Christmas we
>   haven't had to economize.
> HELMER. But you know we can't go squandering.
> NORA. Oh yes, Torvald, we can squander a little now.
>   Can't we?

Verse Drama

Many older plays, including classical Greek drama and much of the work of Shakespeare and his contemporaries, are written at least partly in poetic verse. When you quote a verse drama, you must respect the line endings, just as you do in quoting poetry. The first example here shows a short quotation with slash marks that indicate line endings; the second shows a longer, block quotation in verse form.

> Hamlet's most famous soliloquy begins, "To be, or not to be, that is the question: / Whether 'tis nobler in the mind to suffer / The slings and arrows of outrageous fortune."

Hamlet then begins his most famous soliloquy:

> To be, or not to be, that is the question:
> Whether 'tis nobler in the mind to suffer
> The slings and arrows of outrageous fortune,
> Or to take arms against a sea of troubles,
> And by opposing end them.

Tips for Quoting

- **Double-check the wording, spelling, and punctuation of every quotation you use.** Even if something seems "wrong" in the original source—a nonstandard spelling, a strange mark of punctuation, or even a factual error—resist the urge to correct it. When you put quotation marks around something, you indicate that you are reproducing it exactly as it first appeared. If you feel the need to clarify that an error or inconsistency is not yours, you may follow it by the word *sic* (Latin for *thus*), not italicized, in square brackets. Example:

  The mother in the anonymous poem "Lord Randal" asks her son "wha [sic] met ye there?"

- **Use the shortest quotation you can while still making your point.** Remember, the focus should always be on your own ideas, and the dominant voice should be yours. Don't quote a paragraph from a source when a single sentence contains the heart of what you need. Don't quote a whole sentence when you can simply integrate a few words into one of your own sentences.

- **Never assume a quotation is self-explanatory.** Each time you include a quotation, analyze it and explain why you have quoted it. Remember that your reader may have a different reaction to the quotation than you did.

- **If you are quoting a *character* in a story, play, or poem, be sure to distinguish that character from the *author*.** Hamlet says "To be or not to be," not Shakespeare, and you should make that distinction clear.

- **Take care not to distort the meaning of a quotation.** It is intellectually dishonest to quote an author or speaker out of context or to use ellipses or additions in such a way as to change the meaning or integrity of source material. Treat your sources with the same respect you would want if you were to be quoted in a newspaper or magazine.

MANUSCRIPT FORM

If your instructor gives you directions about what your paper should look like, follow them exactly. If not, the following basic guidelines on manuscript form, recommended by the Modern Language Association of America (MLA), will work well in most instances. The most comprehensive guide to MLA style is *MLA Handbook for Writers of Research Papers*, 7th edition (New York: MLA, 2009). For an online guide to MLA style, see Diana Hacker's *Research and Documentation Online*: http://www.dianahacker.com/resdoc/. The guiding principle here is readability—you want the look of your paper to distract as little as possible from the content.

- **Use plain white paper, black ink, and a standard, easy-to-read font.** To make your paper stand out from the masses, it might seem like a nice touch to use visual design elements like colored or decorated paper, fancy fonts, and so forth. However, your instructor has a lot of reading to do, and anything that distracts or slows that reading down is a minus, not a plus, for your paper. For the same reason, avoid illustrations unless they are needed to clarify a point. Distinguish your paper through content and style, not flashy design.

- **No separate cover page is needed.** Also, don't waste your time and money on report covers or folders unless asked to do so by your instructor. Many instructors, in fact, find covers cumbersome and distracting.

- **Include vital information in the upper left corner of your first page.** This information usually consists of your name, the name of your instructor, the course number of the class, and the date you submit the paper.

- **Center your paper's title.** The title should appear in upper- and lower-case letters, and in the same font as the rest of your paper—not italicized, boldface, or set in quotation marks.

- **Page numbers should appear in the upper right corner of each page.** Do not include the word *page* or the abbreviation *p.* with the page numbers. Use your word processing program's "header" or "running head" feature to include your last name before the page numbers. (See the sample student papers in this book for examples.)

These basic guidelines should carry you through most situations, but if you have any questions regarding format, ask your instructor for his or her preferences.

CHAPTER 3

Common Writing Assignments

SUMMARY

A **summary** is a brief recap of the most important points—plot, character, and so on—in a work of literature. In order to demonstrate that you have understood a story or play, for instance, you may be asked to summarize its plot as homework before class discussions. A summary of Nathaniel Hawthorne's "Young Goodman Brown" follows:

> Set in seventeenth-century Salem, Massachusetts, Nathaniel Hawthorne's "Young Goodman Brown" follows the fortunes of the title character when he leaves his young wife, Faith, for a mysterious rendezvous in a forest at night. The character he meets in the forbidding woods is unnamed, but Hawthorne hints that he may be the Devil himself. As they proceed deeper into the forest on their unspecified but presumably unholy errand, Good-man Brown's misgivings increase, especially when they encounter his fellow townsfolk—people Goodman Brown thought were good Christians—en route to the same meeting. But when they are joined by Faith, Brown recklessly resolves to participate. At the ceremony, the new converts are called forth, but as he and Faith step forward to be anointed in blood, he rebels and urges Faith to resist. Instantly he finds himself alone in the forest, and when he returns to town the next morning, uncertain whether it was all a dream, he finds himself suspicious and wary of his neighbors and his wife. His "Faith" has been corrupted, and to the end of his days he remains a bitter and untrusting man: "his dying hour was gloom."

A summary can be longer or shorter than this example, depending on your purpose. Notice that interpretation is kept to a minimum ("His 'Faith' has been corrupted") and the summary is recounted in the present tense ("he returns to town," "he remains a bitter and untrusting man").

It is rare for a full essay assignment to be based on summary alone. Keep in mind that for most of the papers you write, your readers—your teacher and possibly your classmates—are probably familiar with the literary work you are writing about, and do not need a recap of the entire work. Generally, they need only to be reminded of key points about the text that are most relevant to the argument you are making about it.

While a *summary* is a kind of writing assignment that you may not have to produce very often in a literature course, *summarizing* is a skill you will need to develop. It is a useful skill to be able to focus on the most important parts of a text, knowing what is most vital. Short summaries, either of a work of literature or of critical essays about works of literature, are commonly used as part of the supporting evidence in more complex papers. When you are using secondary sources in a paper about a literary work, chances are that your audience has not read the critical essays you have read. Therefore, you may need to summarize for your readers the arguments of those critical essays.

Often such summaries are only a few sentences in length, and restate the author's thesis, possibly with a few examples of the kind of evidence the author uses to support the thesis. Just as often, you may want to summarize only part of a critical essay, a part that is pertinent to your paper. For example, if you have read an essay about Hawthorne's use of imagery in "Young Goodman Brown," for the purposes of your paper you may need to summarize only the section that deals with the imagery of light and darkness in the story. Ask yourself, "What do my readers need to know to follow my argument, and what evidence do I need to provide to convince them of my point of view?" Summarize accordingly.

EXPLICATION

One common assignment is to perform an **explication** or a **close reading** of a poem or short prose passage. As the word implies, an *explication* takes what is implicit or subtle in a work of literature and makes it explicit and clear. Literary language tends to be densely packed with meaning, and your job as you explicate it is to unfold that meaning and lay it out for your reader. The principal technique of explication is close reading; indeed, explication and close reading are so closely related that the words are often used virtually interchangeably. When you write this sort of paper, you will examine a piece of literature very closely, paying special attention to such elements of the language as sentence structure, style, imagery, **figurative language** (such as similes and metaphors), word choice, and perhaps even grammar and punctuation. The job of an explication is twofold: to point out particular, salient elements of style, and to explain the purpose and effect of these elements within the text.

It is tempting when assigned an explication or close reading to simply walk through a text line by line, pointing out interesting features of style as they occur. A paper written in this way, though, can devolve into little more than summary or restatement of the literature in more prosaic language. A better idea is to isolate the various features of the literature on which you will focus and then deal separately with the specifics and implications of each.

The paper that follows is an example of a student essay that provides an explication of a literary text. First, take a look at Robert Herrick's "Upon Julia's Clothes," and then read the student's paper.

ROBERT HERRICK   [1591–1674]

Upon Julia's Clothes

Whenas in silks my Julia goes,
Then, then (methinks) how sweetly flows
That liquefaction of her clothes.

Next, when I cast mine eyes, and see
That brave vibration each way free,   5
O how that glittering taketh me!

Jessica Barnes
English 108
Professor White
13 March 2008

Poetry in Motion: Herrick's "Upon Julia's Clothes"

In its brief six lines, Robert Herrick's "Upon Julia's Clothes" is a celebration of the physical sensuousness of the speaker's object of desire. The poem is structured like a seashell with two parts. In the first stanza, the speaker makes a seemingly simple observation: when Julia walks past, her silken clothes seem to flow like they're liquid. In the second stanza, though, he provides a second observation: when Julia's body is "each way free" of the clothing, the speaker is completely overtaken by the beauty of Julia's "brave vibration."

Herrick provides several inversions of syntax to place emphasis on certain images. For example, in line 1, Herrick inverts "my Julia goes" with "in silks" to emphasize the importance of "silks" to Julia's sensuality. He creates another inversion in lines 2–3. The sense of the lines is as follows: "Then, then (methinks) that liquefaction of her clothes flows sweetly." Herrick rearranges the line to emphasize the sweetness of the flowing, and to place the emphasis on "flows" and "clothes" at the ends of the lines.

Herrick also provides several changes in the iambic tetrameter meter to create varied lines within the poem's strict form. In line 2, he repeats "then" two times. In doing so, he forces the reader to pause deeply between each "then" and encourages the reader to meditate on the poet's decision to repeat the word in the first place. In line 6, too, Herrick alternately accelerates and decelerates the tempo of the line. The exclamatory "O" at the beginning of the line suggests that the speaker has been utterly charmed by Julia's beauty. It is a long sound that slows the reader down at the beginning of the line; in addition, it provides a stress on the first syllable of the line, instead of an unstressed syllable followed by a stressed one (see, for example, "That **brave** vibration" in line 5). "Glittering" also disrupts the strict tetrameter of the line. Its three syllables are compressed into two brief syllables ("**glitt**ring") so that the next accent can fall on "**tak**eth me," which emphasizes the fact that the speaker is totally overwhelmed by Julia's naked body.

Ultimately, the poem reveals that Julia's beauty is beyond words. We cannot know whether Julia has actually taken her clothes off, or whether she has done so in the imagination of the speaker. Either way, the poem provides many sounds that mirror the "O" of line 6. The end rhyme for all of the lines in the first stanza rhyme with the "O": goes, flows, clothes. Each of these words reinforces the importance of Julia's shimmering beauty, and the power of her movements. The "ee" rhymes at the ends of the lines in stanza 2 — see, free, me — reinforce the idea that Julia's freedom in her nakedness also frees the poet's pleasure in imagining, or seeing, the "brave vibration" of her body.

ANALYSIS

To analyze, by definition, is to take something apart and examine how the individual parts relate to one another and function within the whole. Engineers frequently analyze complex machinery, looking for ways to improve efficiency or performance. In a similar way, you can take apart a piece of literature to study how a particular part of it functions and what that part contributes to the whole. Typical candidates for **literary analysis** include **plot development**, **characterization**, **tone**, **irony**, and **symbols**.

Here is an example of a student essay that provides a close reading. First, take a look at Browning's "My Last Duchess," then read the student's paper.

ROBERT BROWNING   [1812–1889]

My Last Duchess

Ferrara°

That's my last Duchess° painted on the wall,
Looking as if she were alive. I call
That piece a wonder, now: Frà Pandolf's° hands
Worked busily a day, and there she stands.
Will't please you sit and look at her? I said
"Frà Pandolf" by design, for never read
Strangers like you that pictured countenance,
The depth and passion of its earnest glance,
But to myself they turned (since none puts by
The curtain I have drawn for you, but I)
And seemed as they would ask me, if they durst,
How such a glance came there; so, not the first
Are you to turn and ask thus. Sir, 'twas not
Her husband's presence only, called that spot
Of joy into the Duchess' cheek: perhaps
Frà Pandolf chanced to say "Her mantle laps
Over my lady's wrist too much," or "Paint
Must never hope to reproduce the faint
Half-flush that dies along her throat": such stuff
Was courtesy, she thought, and cause enough
For calling up that spot of joy. She had
A heart—how shall I say?—too soon made glad,
Too easily impressed; she liked whate'er
She looked on, and her looks went everywhere.
Sir, 'twas all one! My favor at her breast,
The dropping of the daylight in the West,
The bough of cherries some officious fool
Broke in the orchard for her, the white mule

Ferrara: The poem is based on events that occurred in the life of Alfonso II, duke
of Ferrara in Italy, in the sixteenth century.
1. last Duchess: Ferrara's first wife, Lucrezia, died in 1561 at age seventeen after
three years of marriage.
3. Frà Pandolf: Brother Pandolf, a fictional painter.

She rode with round the terrace—all and each
Would draw from her alike the approving speech,   30
Or blush, at least. She thanked men,—good! but thanked
Somehow—I know not how—as if she ranked
My gift of a nine-hundred-years-old name
With anybody's gift. Who'd stoop to blame
This sort of trifling? Even had you skill   35
In speech—(which I have not)—to make your will
Quite clear to such an one, and say, "Just this
Or that in you disgusts me; here you miss,
Or there exceed the mark"—and if she let
Herself be lessoned so, nor plainly set   40
Her wits to yours, forsooth, and made excuse,
—E'en then would be some stooping; and I choose
Never to stoop. Oh sir, she smiled, no doubt,
Whene'er I passed her; but who passed without
Much the same smile? This grew; I gave commands;   45
Then all smiles stopped together. There she stands
As if alive. Will't please you rise? We'll meet
The company below, then. I repeat,
The Count your master's known munificence
Is ample warrant that no just pretence   50
Of mine for dowry will be disallowed;
Though his fair daughter's self, as I avowed
At starting, is my object. Nay, we'll go
Together down, sir. Notice Neptune, though,
Taming a sea-horse, thought a rarity,   55
Which Claus of Innsbruck° cast in bronze for me!

[1842]

56. Claus of Innsbruck: A fictional sculptor.

Adam Walker

English 203

Professor Blitefield

22 February 2008

Possessed by the Need for Possession:

Browning's "My Last Duchess"

In "My Last Duchess," Robert Browning's duke reveals his feelings of jealousy and betrayal as he discusses the duchess's portrait. In his dramatic monologue, the duke's public persona as an aristocratic gentleman is shattered by the revelations of his actual feelings about his dead duchess. The duke reveals what upsets him most: his former wife's liberal smiles and attentions to others besides himself. With this focus on the duchess's attentions, Browning creates a compelling portrait of a gentleman who could not exert complete control over his former wife, and may fail to control his future wife as well.

The duke repeatedly calls attention to what he sees as the duchess's misinterpretations. The duke imagines the duchess as she sat for Fra Pandolf: "such stuff / Was courtesy, she thought, and cause enough / For calling up that spot of joy" (ll. 19-21). According to the duke, the duchess mistook the painter's attentions as courtesies. Her blush, or "spot of joy" (l. 21) on her cheeks, was too indiscriminate for the duke. The duke admits that the duchess blushed at his own advances, but she also blushed at the painter, the "dropping of the daylight in the West," (l. 26), a bough of cherries, and a white mule. The duchess's gaze is an indiscriminate one: she appreciates whatever pleases her, whether it be human, animal, or organic. This infuriates the duke, who thinks that his "nine-hundred-years-old name" (l. 33) ought to make him more valuable in the eyes of the duchess.

Eventually, the duke restricts the duchess's blushes with commands: "This grew; I gave commands; / Then all smiles stopped together. There she stands / As if alive" (ll. 45-47). These lines are concise and quick compared with the rhetoric of the other lines in the poem. Even so, they are in some ways the most important. What made the smiles stop? Was the duchess silenced in life? Or was it her death that stopped the smiling? And why does the duke need this portrait that resembles the duchess when she was alive?

Walker 2

Ultimately, the showing of the portrait is a way for the duke to show his possessions — and his command of his possessions — to the envoy of the Count. As the duke invites the envoy to come downstairs, he already characterizes his future bride as a kind of possession:

> I repeat,
> The Count your master's known munificence
> Is ample warrant that no just pretence
> Of mine for dowry will be disallowed;
> Though his fair daughter's self, as I avowed
> At starting, is my object. (ll. 48-53)

After alluding to the generous dowry that he will receive, the duke checks himself by saying that it is "his fair daughter's self" that he has found so compelling. Even so, the duke has started to limit and control the status of his future bride, suggesting that he will exert the same controls on her that he exerted on his former wife. In the end, she runs the same risk of becoming a sea horse that requires Neptune's taming.

COMPARISON AND CONTRAST

Another common paper assignment is the **comparison and contrast** essay. You might be asked to draw comparisons and contrasts within a single work of literature — say, between two characters in a story or play. Even more common is an assignment that asks you to compare and contrast a particular element — a character, setting, style, tone, and so on — in two or more stories, poems, or plays. A *comparison* emphasizes the similarities between two or more items, while a *contrast* highlights their differences. Though some papers do both, it is typical for an essay to emphasize one or the other.

If you are allowed to choose the works of literature for a comparison and contrast paper, take care to select works that have enough in common to make such a comparison interesting and valid. Even if Henrik Ibsen's *A Doll House* and Shirley Jackson's "The Lottery" are your favorites, it is difficult to imagine a well-focused paper comparing these two, as they share virtually nothing in terms of authorship, history, theme, or style. It would make far more sense to select two seventeenth-century poems or two love stories.

The paper that follows compares Robert Browning's "My Last Duchess" and Christina Rossetti's "After Death." First, read Rossetti's poem, then read the student paper.

CHRISTINA ROSSETTI   [1830–1894]

After Death

The curtains were half drawn, the floor was swept
   And strewn with rushes, rosemary and may
Lay thick upon the bed on which I lay,
Where through the lattice ivy-shadows crept.
He leaned above me, thinking that I slept   5
   And could not hear him; but I heard him say,
   'Poor child, poor child': and as he turned away
Came a deep silence, and I knew he wept.
He did not touch the shroud, or raise the fold
   That hid my face, or take my hand in his,   10
    Or ruffle the smooth pillows for my head:
    He did not love me living; but once dead
   He pitied me; and very sweet it is
To know he still is warm though I am cold.

Todd Bowen
English 215
Professor Harrison
12 May 2008

Speakers for the Dead:
Narrators in "My Last Duchess"
and "After Death"

In "My Last Duchess," Robert Browning creates a duke whose tight
control over his wife — and his preoccupation with his own noble rank —
reveal a misogynistic character. Browning's dramatic monologue stands in
stark contrast to Christina Rossetti's "After Death," a sonnet in which the
speaker comes back from the dead to reveal what she observes about her lover.
When paired together, these poems speak to one another in a time period that
seemed to have a gothic obsession with the death of young women.

In their style and structure, Browning and Rossetti create completely
different portraits of women after death. In "My Last Duchess," the duke uses
the actual portrait of his dead wife to create a portrait in words of a woman
that smiled too liberally at men who fawned over her. The duke says, "She
had / A heart — how shall I say? — too soon made glad, / Too easily
impressed; she liked whate'er / She looked on, and her looks went everywhere"
(ll. 21-24). Throughout his long dramatic monologue, the duke meditates on
several moments when the duchess betrays him by smiling at others; however,
we as readers never get to hear the duchess's side of the story.

In Rossetti's "After Death," however, the tables are turned: the dead
woman gets to speak back to the man who performs his grief over her death.
In doing so, she carefully observes the behavior of her lover, who thinks that
she is merely a lifeless corpse. In each line of the small sonnet, the speaker
observes the man as he leans above her, says "'Poor child, poor child'" (l. 7),
then turns away without actually touching her body. Even so, the woman
suggests that this is an improvement from when she was alive: "He did not
love me living; but once dead / He pitied me" (ll. 12-13). The speaker's final
couplet is especially chilling: "and very sweet is / To know he still is warm
though I am cold" (ll. 13-14). The speaker says that it is "sweet" to know

that the man has outlived her. She doesn't explain this sweetness, but perhaps it is because she can observe his emotion in a way that she never could have while she was alive.

When read together, Rossetti's "After Death" and Browning's "My Last Duchess" function as companion pieces, each speaking to the other in a kind of call-and-response. Browning's duke shuts down any speech beyond his own, talking at length in the silence of the portrait and the visitor who looks at it. His story is the only story that he wants to present, even if his speech reveals his own shortcomings. Rossetti's woman provides an alternative perspective of death and mourning as the woman speaks from the dead to reveal the shortcomings of the man who mourns her. Both poems provide chilling perspectives on death, mourning, and marriage in the Victorian period.

ESSAY EXAMS

The key to getting through the potentially stressful situation of an essay exam is to be prepared and to know what will be expected of you.

Preparation takes two forms: knowing the material and anticipating the questions. Knowing the material starts with keeping up with all reading and homework assignments throughout the term. You can't possibly read several weeks' or months' worth of material the night before the test and hope to remember it all. The days before the test should be used not for catching up but for review—revisiting the readings, skimming or rereading key passages, and studying your class notes. It's best to break up study sessions into manageable blocks if possible. Reviewing for two hours a night for three nights before the exam will be far more effective than a single six-hour cram session on the eve of the test.

Anticipating the questions that might be on the exam is a bit trickier, but it can be done. What themes and issues have come up again and again in class lectures or discussions? What patterns do you see in your class notes? What points did your instructor stress? These are the topics most likely to appear on the exam. Despite what it might seem like, it is very rare that an instructor poses intentionally obscure exam questions in an attempt to trip students up or expose their ignorance. Most often, the instructor is providing you with an opportunity to demonstrate what you know, and you should be ready to take that opportunity. You can't, of course, second-guess your instructor perfectly and know for sure what will be on the test, but you can spend some time in advance thinking about what sorts of questions you are likely to encounter and how you would answer them.

Your exam may be **open-book** or **closed-book**; find out in advance which it will be, so you can plan and study accordingly. In an *open-book* test, you are allowed to use your textbook during the exam. This is a big advantage, obviously, as it allows you access to specific evidence, including quotations, to support your points. If you know the exam is going to be open-book, you might also jot down any important notes in the book itself, where you can find them readily if you need them. Use your textbook sparingly, though—just enough to find the evidence you know to be there. Don't waste time browsing the literature hoping to find inspiration or ideas. For a *closed-book* exam, you have to rely on your memory alone. But you should still try to be as specific as possible in your references to the literature, using character names, recalling plot elements, and so forth.

When you sit down to take the exam, you may have the urge to start writing right away, since your time is limited. Suppress that urge and read through the entire exam first, paying special attention to the instruction portion. Often there will be choices to make, such as "Answer two of the following three questions" or "Select a single poem as the basis of your answer." If you miss such cues, you may find yourself racing to write three essays and running out of time or discussing several poems shallowly instead of one in depth. Once you are certain what is expected of you, take a few more minutes to plan your answers before you start writing. A few jotted notes or an informal outline may take a moment, but it will likely save you time as you write. If you will be writing more than one essay, take care not to repeat yourself or to write more than one essay about any one piece of literature. The idea is to show your instructor your mastery of the course, and to do so effectively you should demonstrate breadth of knowledge.

When you do begin writing, bear in mind that instructors have different expectations for exam answers than they do for essays written outside of class. They know that in timed exams you have no time for research or extensive revisions. Clarity and concision are the keys; elegant prose style is not expected (though, of course, it will come as a pleasant surprise if you can manage it). Effective essay answers are often more formulaic than other sorts of effective writing, relying on the schematic of a straightforward introduction, simple body paragraphs, and a brief conclusion.

Your introduction should be simple and to the point. A couple of sentences is generally all that is needed, and these should avoid rhetorical flourishes or digressions. Often the best strategy is to parrot back the instructions as an opening statement. Imagine, for instance, you were asked to choose from among several options, including, "Select two poems by different poets, each of which deals with the theme of time, and compare how the authors present this theme." A possible beginning might be:

> Shakespeare's Sonnet 73 (That time of year thou mayst in me behold) and Herrick's "To the Virgins, to Make Much of Time" both deal with the theme of time. Though there are important differences in their focus and style, both poems urge their readers to love well and make the most of the time they have left.

Although this is not shatteringly original, and the prose style is blunt and not particularly memorable, this introduction does its job. It lets the reader know which question the student is answering, which poems will be examined, and what the general point of the essay will be.

Body paragraphs for essay answers should also be simple, and will often, though not always, be briefer than they would be in an essay you worked on at home. They should still be as specific as possible, making reference to and perhaps even quoting the literature to illustrate your points. Just as in a more fully developed essay, try to avoid dwelling in generalities; use specific examples and evidence. Following the introduction above, for instance, you might expect one paragraph discussing the theme of time in Shakespeare's poem, another paragraph doing the same for Herrick's, and perhaps a third making explicit the connections between the two. Conclusions for essay exams are usually brief, just a sentence or two of summary.

Finally, take a watch with you on exam day and keep a close eye on the time. Use all the time you are given and budget it carefully. If you have an hour to write two answers, don't spend forty-five minutes on the first. Even though you will likely be pressed for time, save a few minutes at the end to proofread your answers. Make any corrections as neatly and legibly as possible. Watch the time, but try not to watch your classmates' progress. Keep focused on your own process. Just because someone else is using his or her book a lot, you shouldn't feel you need to do the same. If someone finishes early and leaves, don't take this as a sign that you are running behind or that you are less efficient or smart than that person. Students who don't make full use of the exam time are often underprepared; they tend to write vague and underdeveloped answers and should not be your role models.

CHAPTER 4

Writing about Stories

Fiction has long been broken down and discussed in terms of specific elements common to all stories, and chances are you will be focusing on one or more of these when you write an essay about a story.

ELEMENTS OF FICTION

The **elements of fiction** most commonly identified are **plot, character, point of view, setting, theme, symbol**, and **style**. If you find yourself wondering what to write about a story, a good place to begin is isolating these elements and seeing how they work on a reader and how they combine to create the unique artifact that is a particular story.

Plot

While on some level we all read stories to find out what happens next, in truth **plot** is usually the least interesting of the elements of fiction. Students who have little experience writing about fiction tend to spend too much time retelling the plot. You can avoid this by bearing in mind that your readers will also have read the literature in question and don't need a thorough replay of what happened. In general, all readers need are small reminders of the key points of plot about which you will write, and these should not be self-standing but rather should serve as springboards into analysis and discussion. Still, there are times when writing about the plot makes sense, especially when the plot surprises your expectations by, for instance, rearranging the chronology of events or otherwise presenting things in nonrealistic ways. When this happens in a story, the plot may indeed prove fertile ground for analysis and may be the basis of an interesting paper.

Characters

Many interesting essays analyze the actions, motivations, and development of individual characters. How does the author reveal a character to the reader? How does a character grow and develop over the course of a story? Readers have to carefully examine what insights the text provides about a character, but sometimes readers have to consider what's left out. What does the reader have to infer about the character that isn't explicitly written? What does the character refrain from saying? What secrets do characters keep from others, or from themselves? These questions can be fertile ground for analysis. Although the most obvious character to write about is usually the **protagonist**, don't let your imagination stop there. Often the **antagonist** or even a minor character can be an interesting object of study. Keep in mind, too, that characters can start out as antagonistic figures and experience a transformation in their own eyes, the eyes of other characters, or the eyes of the narrator. Your job as a writer is to consider these transformations and try to understand why a text explores these complex character developments. Usually less has been said and written about less prominent characters, so you will be more free to create your own interpretations. (Playwright Tom Stoppard wrote a very successful full-length play entitled *Rosencrantz and Guildenstern Are Dead* about two of the least developed characters in *Hamlet*.)

Point of View

Related to character is the issue of point of view. The perspective from which a story is told can make a big difference in how we perceive it. Sometimes a story is told in the *first person*, from the point of view of one of the characters. Whether this is a major or a minor character, we must always remember that **first-person narrators** can be unreliable, as they do not have access to all vital information, and their own agendas can often skew the way they see events. The **narrator** of Edgar Allan Poe's "The Cask of Amontillado" seeks to gain sympathy for a hideous act of revenge, giving us a glimpse into a deeply disturbed mind. A **third-person narrator** may be **omniscient**, knowing everything pertinent to a story; or limited, knowing, for instance, the thoughts and motives of the protagonist but not of any of the other characters. As you read a story, ask yourself what the point of view contributes and why the author may have chosen to present the story from a particular perspective.

Setting

Sometimes a **setting** is merely the backdrop for a story, but often place plays an important role in our understanding of a work. John Updike chooses a small, conservative New England town as the setting of his story "A & P." It is the perfect milieu for an exploration of values and class interaction, and the story would have a very different feel and meaning if it had been set, say, in New York City. Ask yourself as you read how significant a setting is and what it adds to the meaning of a story. Remember that setting refers to time as well as place. "A & P" is about three young women walking into a small-town grocery store wearing only bathing suits, an action more shocking when the story was written in 1961 than it would be now (although it would doubtless still raise eyebrows in many places).

Theme

All **short stories** have at least one theme — an abstract concept such as *love, war, friendship, revenge, art*, and so forth — brought to life and made real through the plot, characters, and so on. Identifying a theme or themes is one of the first keys to understanding a story, but it is not the end point. Pay some attention to how the theme is developed. Is it blatant or subtle? What actions, events, or symbols make the theme apparent to you? Generally, the driving force of a story is the author's desire to convey something *about* a particular theme, to make readers think and feel in a certain way. First ask yourself what the author seems to be saying about love or war or whatever themes you have noted; second, whether you agree with the author's perceptions; and finally, why or why not.

Symbolism

Some students get frustrated when their instructors or their class-mates begin to talk about **symbolism**. How do we know that an author intended a symbolic reading? Maybe that flower is just a real flower, not a stand-in for youth or for life and regeneration as some readers insist. And even if it is a symbol, how do we know we are reading it correctly? Careful writers choose their words and images for maximum impact, filling them with as much meaning as possible and inviting their readers to interpret them. The more prominent an image in a story, the more likely it is meant to be read symbolically. When John Steinbeck entitles his story "The Chrysanthemums," we would do well to ask if the flowers are really just plants or if we are being asked to look for a greater significance.

Style

The final element of fiction we will isolate here is **style**, sometimes spoken of under the heading of tone or language. A text may strike you as sad or lighthearted, formal or casual. It may make you feel nostalgic, or it may make your heart race with excitement. Somewhat more diffi-cult, though, is isolating the elements of language that contribute to a particular tone or effect. Look for characteristic stylistic elements that create these effects. Is the diction elevated and difficult, or ordinary and simple? Are the sentences long and complex, or short and to the point? Is there dialogue? If so, how do the characters who speak this dialogue come across? Does the style stay consistent throughout the story, or does it change? What does the author leave out? Paying close attention to linguistic matters like these will take you far in your understanding of how a particular story achieves its effect.

STORIES FOR ANALYSIS

The two stories that follow, Kate Chopin's "The Story of an Hour" and Charlotte Perkins Gilman's "The Yellow Wallpaper," explore issues of women's identity and freedom. The questions after the stories ask you to tease out how the elements of fiction work in them.

KATE CHOPIN [1851–1904]

The Story of an Hour

Knowing that Mrs. Mallard was afflicted with a heart trouble, great care was taken to break to her as gently as possible the news of her husband's death.

It was her sister Josephine who told her, in broken sentences; veiled hints that revealed in half concealing. Her husband's friend Richards was there, too, near her. It was he who had been in the newspaper office when intelligence of the railroad disaster was received, with Brently Mallard's name leading the list of "killed." He had only taken the time to assure himself of its truth by a second telegram, and had hastened to forestall any less careful, less tender friend in bearing the sad message.

She did not hear the story as many women have heard the same, with a paralyzed inability to accept its significance. She wept at once, with sudden, wild abandonment, in her sister's arms. When the storm of grief had spent itself she went away to her room alone. She would have no one follow her.

There stood, facing the open window, a comfortable, roomy armchair. Into this she sank, pressed down by a physical exhaustion that haunted her body and seemed to reach into her soul.

She could see in the open square before her house the tops of trees that were all aquiver with the new spring life. The delicious breath of rain was in the air. In the street below a peddler was crying his wares. The notes of a distant song which some one was singing reached her faintly, and countless sparrows were twittering in the eaves.

There were patches of blue sky showing here and there through the clouds that had met and piled one above the other in the west facing her window.

She sat with her head thrown back upon the cushion of the chair, quite motionless, except when a sob came up into her throat and shook her, as a child who had cried itself to sleep continues to sob in its dreams.

She was young, with a fair, calm face, whose lines bespoke repression and even a certain strength. But now there was a dull stare in her eyes, whose gaze was fixed away off yonder on one of those patches of blue sky. It was not a glance of reflection, but rather indicated a suspension of intelligent thought.

There was something coming to her and she was waiting for it, fearfully. What was it? She did not know; it was too subtle and elusive to name. But she felt it, creeping out of the sky, reaching toward her through the sounds, the scents, the color that filled the air.

Now her bosom rose and fell tumultuously. She was beginning to recognize this thing that was approaching to possess her, and she was striving to beat it back with her will—as powerless as her two white slender hands would have been.

When she abandoned herself a little whispered word escaped her slightly parted lips. She said it over and over under her breath: "free, free, free!" The vacant stare and the look of terror that had followed it went from her eyes. They stayed keen and bright. Her pulses beat fast, and the coursing blood warmed and relaxed every inch of her body.

She did not stop to ask if it were or were not a monstrous joy that held her. A clear and exalted perception enabled her to dismiss the suggestion as trivial.

She knew that she would weep again when she saw the kind, tender hands folded in death; the face that had never looked save with love upon her, fixed and gray and dead. But she saw beyond that bitter moment a long procession of years to come that would belong to her absolutely. And she opened and spread her arms out to them in welcome.

There would be no one to live for her during those coming years: she would live for herself. There would be no powerful will bending hers in that blind persistence with which men and women believe they have a right to impose a private will upon a fellow-creature. A kind intention or a cruel intention made the act seem no less a crime as she looked upon it in that brief moment of illumination.

And yet she had loved him—sometimes. Often she had not. What did it matter! What could love, the unsolved mystery, count for in face of this possession of self-assertion which she suddenly recognized as the strongest impulse of her being!

"Free! Body and soul free!" she kept whispering.

Josephine was kneeling before the closed door with her lips to the keyhole, imploring for admission. "Louise, open the door! I beg; open the door—you will make yourself ill. What are you doing, Louise? For heaven's sake open the door."

"Go away. I am not making myself ill." No; she was drinking in a very elixir of life through that open window.

Her fancy was running riot along those days ahead of her. Spring days, and summer days, and all sorts of days that would be her own. She breathed a quick prayer that life might be long. It was only yesterday she had thought with a shudder that life might be long.

She arose at length and opened the door to her sister's importunities. There was a feverish triumph in her eyes, and she carried herself unwittingly like a goddess of Victory. She clasped her sister's waist, and together they descended the stairs. Richards stood waiting for them at the bottom.

Some one was opening the front door with a latchkey. It was Brently Mallard who entered, a little travel-stained, composedly carrying his gripsack and umbrella. He had been far from the scene of accident, and did not even know there had been one. He stood amazed at Josephine's piercing cry; at Richards' quick motion to screen him from the view of his wife.

But Richards was too late.

When the doctors came they said she had died of heart disease — of joy that kills.

[1894]

CHARLOTTE PERKINS GILMAN   [1860–1935]

The Yellow Wallpaper

It is very seldom that mere ordinary people like John and myself secure ancestral halls for the summer.

A colonial mansion, a hereditary estate, I would say a haunted house and reach the height of romantic felicity — but that would be asking too much of fate!

Still I will proudly declare that there is something queer about it.

Else, why should it be let so cheaply? And why have stood so long untenanted?

John laughs at me, of course, but one expects that in marriage.

John is practical in the extreme. He has no patience with faith, an intense horror of superstition, and he scoffs openly at any talk of things not to be felt and seen and put down in figures.

John is a physician, and *perhaps* — (I would not say it to a living soul, of course, but this is dead paper and a great relief to my mind) — *perhaps* that is one reason I do not get well faster.

You see, he does not believe I am sick!

And what can one do?

If a physician of high standing, and one's own husband, assures friends and relatives that there is really nothing the matter with one but temporary nervous depression — a slight hysterical tendency — what is one to do?

My brother is also a physician, and also of high standing, and he says the same thing.

So I take phosphates or phosphites — whichever it is, and tonics, and journeys, and air, and exercise, and am absolutely forbidden to "work" until I am well again.

Personally, I disagree with their ideas.

Personally, I believe that congenial work, with excitement and change, would do me good.

But what is one to do?

I did write for a while in spite of them; but it *does* exhaust me a good deal — having to be so sly about it, or else meet with heavy opposition.

I sometimes fancy that in my condition if I had less opposition and more society and stimulus — but John says the very worst thing I can do is to think about my condition, and I confess it always makes me feel bad.

So I will let it alone and talk about the house.

The most beautiful place! It is quite alone, standing well back from the road, quite three miles from the village. It makes me think of English places that you read about, for there are hedges and walls and gates that lock, and lots of separate little houses for the gardeners and people.

There is a *delicious* garden! I never saw such a garden — large and shady, full of box-bordered paths, and lined with long grape-covered arbors with seats under them.

There were greenhouses, too, but they are all broken now.

There was some legal trouble, I believe, something about the heirs and co-heirs; anyhow, the place has been empty for years.

That spoils my ghostliness, I am afraid, but I don't care — there is something strange about the house — I can feel it.

I even said so to John one moonlight evening, but he said what I felt was a *draught*, and shut the window.

I get unreasonably angry with John sometimes. I'm sure I never used to be so sensitive. I think it is due to this nervous condition.

But John says if I feel so, I shall neglect proper self-control; so I take pains to control myself — before him, at least, and that makes me very tired.

I don't like our room a bit. I wanted one downstairs that opened on the piazza and had roses all over the window, and such pretty old-fashioned chintz hangings! but John would not hear of it.

He said there was only one window and not room for two beds, and no near room for him if he took another.

He is very careful and loving, and hardly lets me stir without special direction.

I have a schedule prescription for each hour in the day; he takes all care from me, and so I feel basely ungrateful not to value it more.

He said we came here solely on my account, that I was to have perfect rest and all the air I could get. "Your exercise depends on your strength, my dear," said he, "and your food somewhat on your appetite; but air you can absorb all the time." So we took the nursery at the top of the house.

It is a big, airy room, the whole floor nearly, with windows that look all ways, and air and sunshine galore. It was nursery first and then play-room and gymnasium, I should judge; for the windows are barred for little children, and there are rings and things in the walls.

The paint and paper look as if a boys' school had used it. It is stripped off—the paper—in great patches all around the head of my bed, about as far as I can reach, and in a great place on the other side of the room low down. I never saw a worse paper in my life.

One of those sprawling flamboyant patterns committing every artistic sin.

It is dull enough to confuse the eye in following, pronounced enough to constantly irritate and provoke study, and when you follow the lame uncertain curves for a little distance they suddenly commit suicide—plunge off at outrageous angles, destroy themselves in unheard of contradictions.

The color is repellant, almost revolting; a smouldering unclean yellow, strangely faded by the slow-turning sunlight.

It is a dull yet lurid orange in some places, a sickly sulphur tint in others.

No wonder the children hated it! I should hate it myself if I had to live in this room long.

There comes John, and I must put this away,—he hates to have me write a word.

We have been here two weeks, and I haven't felt like writing before, since that first day.

I am sitting by the window now, up in this atrocious nursery, and there is nothing to hinder my writing as much as I please, save lack of strength.

John is away all day, and even some nights when his cases are serious.

I am glad my case is not serious!

But these nervous troubles are dreadfully depressing.

John does not know how much I really suffer. He knows there is no *reason* to suffer, and that satisfies him.

Of course it is only nervousness. It does weigh on me so not to do my duty in any way!

I meant to be such a help to John, such a real rest and comfort, and here I am a comparative burden already!

Nobody would believe what an effort it is to do what little I am able, — to dress and entertain, and order things.

It is fortunate Mary is so good with the baby. Such a dear baby!

And yet I *cannot* be with him, it makes me so nervous.

I suppose John never was nervous in his life. He laughs at me so about this wallpaper!

At first he meant to repaper the room, but afterward he said that I was letting it get the better of me, and that nothing was worse for a nervous patient than to give way to such fancies.

He said that after the wallpaper was changed it would be the heavy bedstead, and then the barred windows, and then that gate at the head of the stairs, and so on.

"You know the place is doing you good," he said, "and really, dear, I don't care to renovate the house just for a three months' rental."

"Then do let us go downstairs," I said, "there are such pretty rooms there."

Then he took me in his arms and called me a blessed little goose, and said he would go down cellar, if I wished, and have it white-washed into the bargain.

But he is right enough about the beds and windows and things.

It is an airy and comfortable room as anyone need wish, and, of course, I would not be so silly as to make him uncomfortable just for a whim.

I'm really getting quite fond of the big room, all but that horrid paper.

Out of one window I can see the garden, those mysterious deep-shaded arbors, the riotous old-fashioned flowers, and bushes and gnarly trees.

Out of another I get a lovely view of the bay and a little private wharf belonging to the estate. There is a beautiful shaded lane that runs down there from the house. I always fancy I see people walking in these numerous paths and arbors, but John has cautioned me not to give way to fancy in the least. He says that with my imaginative power and habit of story-making, a nervous weakness like mine is sure to lead to all manner of excited fancies, and that I ought to use my will and good sense to check the tendency. So I try.

I think sometimes that if I were only well enough to write a little it would relieve the press of ideas and rest me.

But I find I get pretty tired when I try.

It is so discouraging not to have any advice and companionship about my work. When I get really well, John says we will ask Cousin Henry and Julia down for a long visit; but he says he would as soon put fireworks in my pillow-case as to let me have those stimulating people about now.

I wish I could get well faster.

But I must not think about that. This paper looks to me as if it *knew* what a vicious influence it had!

There is a recurrent spot where the pattern lolls like a broken neck and two bulbous eyes stare at you upside down.

I get positively angry with the impertinence of it and the ever-lastingness. Up and down and sideways they crawl, and those absurd, unblinking eyes are everywhere. There is one place where two breadths didn't match, and the eyes go all up and down the line, one a little higher than the other.

I never saw so much expression in an inanimate thing before, and we all know how much expression they have! I used to lie awake as a child and get more entertainment and terror out of blank walls and plain furniture than most children could find in a toy-store.

I remember what a kindly wink the knobs of our big, old bureau used to have, and there was one chair that always seemed like a strong friend.

I used to feel that if any of the other things looked too fierce I could always hop into that chair and be safe.

The furniture in this room is no worse than inharmonious, however, for we had to bring it all from downstairs. I suppose when this was used as a playroom they had to take the nursery things out, and no wonder! I never saw such ravages as the children have made here.

The wallpaper, as I said before, is torn off in spots, and it sticketh closer than a brother—they must have had perseverance as well as hatred.

Then the floor is scratched and gouged and splintered, the plaster itself is dug out here and there, and this great heavy bed, which is all we found in the room, looks as if it had been through the wars.

But I don't mind it a bit—only the paper.

There comes John's sister. Such a dear girl as she is, and so careful of me! I must not let her find me writing.

She is a perfect and enthusiastic housekeeper, and hopes for no better profession. I verily believe she thinks it is the writing which made me sick!

But I can write when she is out, and see her a long way off from these windows.

There is one that commands the road, a lovely shaded winding road, and one that just looks off over the country. A lovely country, too, full of great elms and velvet meadows.

This wallpaper has a kind of sub-pattern in a different shade, a particularly irritating one, for you can only see it in certain lights, and not clearly then.

But in the places where it isn't faded and where the sun is just so—I can see a strange, provoking, formless sort of figure, that seems to skulk about behind that silly and conspicuous front design.

There's sister on the stairs!

Well, the Fourth of July is over! The people are all gone and I am tired out. John thought it might do me good to see a little company, so we just had mother and Nellie and the children down for a week.

Of course I didn't do a thing. Jennie sees to everything now.

But it tired me all the same.

John says if I don't pick up faster he shall send me to Weir Mitchell° in the fall.

But I don't want to go there at all. I had a friend who was in his hands once, and she says he is just like John and my brother, only more so!

Besides, it is such an undertaking to go so far.

I don't feel as if it was worthwhile to turn my hand over for anything, and I'm getting dreadfully fretful and querulous.

I cry at nothing, and cry most of the time.

Of course I don't when John is here, or anybody else, but when I am alone.

And I am alone a good deal just now. John is kept in town very often by serious cases, and Jennie is good and lets me alone when I want her to.

So I walk a little in the garden or down that lovely lane, sit on the porch under the roses, and lie down up here a good deal.

I'm getting really fond of the room in spite of the wallpaper. Perhaps *because* of the wallpaper.

It dwells in my mind so!

I lie here on this great immovable bed—it is nailed down, I believe—and follow that pattern about by the hour. It is as good as gymnastics, I assure you. I start, we'll say, at the bottom, down in the corner over there where it has not been touched, and I determine for the thousandth time that I *will* follow that pointless pattern to some sort of a conclusion.

Weir Mitchell: Dr. S. Weir Mitchell (1829–1914) was an American neurologist and author who advocated "rest cures" for nervous illnesses.

I know a little of the principle of design, and I know this thing was not arranged on any laws of radiation, or alternation, or repetition, or symmetry, or anything else that I ever heard of.

It is repeated, of course, by the breadths, but not otherwise.

Looked at in one way each breadth stands alone, the bloated curves and flourishes—a kind of "debased Romanesque" with *delirium tremens*—go waddling up and down in isolated columns of fatuity.

But, on the other hand, they connect diagonally, and the sprawling outlines run off in great slanting waves of optic horror, like a lot of wallowing sea-weeds in full chase.

The whole thing goes horizontally, too, at least it seems so, and I exhaust myself in trying to distinguish the order of its going in that direction.

They have used a horizontal breadth for a frieze, and that adds wonderfully to the confusion.

There is one end of the room where it is almost intact, and there, when the crosslights fade and the low sun shines directly upon it, I can almost fancy radiation after all,—the interminable grotesques seem to form around a common centre and rush off in headlong plunges of equal distraction.

It makes me tired to follow it. I will take a nap I guess.

I don't know why I should write this.

I don't want to.

I don't feel able.

And I know John would think it absurd. But I *must* say what I feel and think in some way—it is such a relief!

But the effort is getting to be greater than the relief.

Half the time now I am awfully lazy, and lie down ever so much.

John says I mustn't lose my strength, and has me take cod liver oil and lots of tonics and things, to say nothing of ale and wine and rare meat.

Dear John! He loves me very dearly, and hates to have me sick. I tried to have a real earnest reasonable talk with him the other day, and tell him how I wish he would let me go and make a visit to Cousin Henry and Julia.

But he said I wasn't able to go, nor able to stand it after I got there; and I did not make out a very good case for myself, for I was crying before I had finished.

It is getting to be a great effort for me to think straight. Just this nervous weakness I suppose.

And dear John gathered me up in his arms, and just carried me upstairs and laid me on the bed, and sat by me and read to me till it tired my head.

He said I was his darling and his comfort and all he had, and that I must take care of myself for his sake, and keep well.

He says no one but myself can help me out of it, that I must use my will and self-control and not let any silly fancies run away with me.

There's one comfort, the baby is well and happy, and does not have to occupy this nursery with the horrid wallpaper.

If we had not used it, that blessed child would have! What a fortunate escape! Why, I wouldn't have a child of mine, an impressionable little thing, live in such a room for worlds.

I never thought of it before, but it is lucky that John kept me here after all, I can stand it so much easier than a baby, you see.

Of course I never mention it to them any more—I am too wise, but I keep watch of it all the same.

There are things in the wallpaper that nobody knows but me, or ever will.

Behind that outside pattern the dim shapes get clearer every day.

It is always the same shape, only very numerous.

And it is like a woman stooping down and creeping about behind that pattern. I don't like it a bit. I wonder—I begin to think—I wish John would take me away from here!

It is so hard to talk with John about my case, because he is so wise, and because he loves me so.

But I tried it last night.

It was moonlight. The moon shines in all around just as the sun does.

I hate to see it sometimes, it creeps so slowly, and always comes in by one window or another.

John was asleep and I hated to waken him, so I kept still and watched the moonlight on that undulating wallpaper till I felt creepy.

The faint figure behind seemed to shake the pattern, just as if she wanted to get out.

I got up softly and went to feel and see if the paper *did* move, and when I came back John was awake.

"What is it, little girl?" he said. "Don't go walking about like that—you'll get cold."

I thought it was a good time to talk, so I told him that I really was not gaining here, and that I wished he would take me away.

"Why, darling!" said he, "our lease will be up in three weeks, and I can't see how to leave before.

"The repairs are not done at home, and I cannot possibly leave town just now. Of course if you were in any danger, I could and would, but you really are better, dear, whether you can see it or not. I am a doctor, dear, and I know. You are gaining flesh and color, your appetite is better, I feel really much easier about you."

"I don't weigh a bit more," said I, "nor as much; and my appetite may be better in the evening when you are here but it is worse in the morning when you are away!"

"Bless her little heart!" said he with a big hug, "she shall be as sick as she pleases! But now let's improve the shining hours by going to sleep, and talk about it in the morning!"

"And you won't go away?" I asked gloomily.

"Why, how can I, dear? It is only three weeks more and then we will take a nice little trip of a few days while Jennie is getting the house ready. Really dear you are better!"

"Better in body perhaps—" I began, and stopped short, for he sat up straight and looked at me with such a stern, reproachful look that I could not say another word.

"My darling," said he, "I beg you, for my sake and for our child's sake, as well as for your own, that you will never for one instant let that idea enter your mind! There is nothing so dangerous, so fascinating, to a temperament like yours. It is a false and foolish fancy. Can you trust me as a physician when I tell you so?"

So of course I said no more on that score, and we went to sleep before long. He thought I was asleep first, but I wasn't, and lay there for hours trying to decide whether that front pattern and the back pattern really did move together or separately.

On a pattern like this, by daylight, there is a lack of sequence, a defiance of law, that is a constant irritant to a normal mind.

The color is hideous enough, and unreliable enough, and infuriating enough, but the pattern is torturing.

You think you have mastered it, but just as you get well underway in following, it turns a back-somersault and there you are. It slaps you in the face, knocks you down, and tramples upon you. It is like a bad dream.

The outside pattern is a florid arabesque, reminding one of a fungus. If you can imagine a toadstool in joints, an interminable string of toadstools, budding and sprouting in endless convolutions—why, that is something like it.

That is, sometimes!

There is one marked peculiarity about this paper, a thing nobody seems to notice but myself, and that is that it changes as the light changes.

When the sun shoots in through the east window—I always watch for that first long, straight ray—it changes so quickly that I never can quite believe it.

That is why I watch it always.

By moonlight—the moon shines in all night when there is a moon—I wouldn't know it was the same paper.

At night in any kind of light, in twilight, candlelight, lamplight, and worst of all by moonlight, it becomes bars! The outside pattern I mean, and the woman behind it is as plain as can be.

I didn't realize for a long time what the thing was that showed behind, that dim sub-pattern, but now I am quite sure it is a woman.

By daylight she is subdued, quiet. I fancy it is the pattern that keeps her so still. It is so puzzling. It keeps me quiet by the hour.

I lie down ever so much now. John says it is good for me, and to sleep all I can.

Indeed he started the habit by making me lie down for an hour after each meal.

It is a very bad habit I am convinced, for you see I don't sleep.

And that cultivates deceit, for I don't tell them I'm awake—O, no!

The fact is I am getting a little afraid of John.

He seems very queer sometimes, and even Jennie has an inexplicable look.

It strikes me occasionally, just as a scientific hypothesis,—that perhaps it is the paper!

I have watched John when he did not know I was looking, and come into the room suddenly on the most innocent excuses, and I've caught him several times *looking at the paper!* And Jennie too. I caught Jennie with her hand on it once.

She didn't know I was in the room, and when I asked her in a quiet, a very quiet voice, with the most restrained manner possible, what she was doing with the paper—she turned around as if she had been caught stealing, and looked quite angry—asked me why I should frighten her so!

Then she said that the paper stained everything it touched, that she had found yellow smooches on all my clothes and John's, and she wished we would be more careful!

Did not that sound innocent? But I know she was studying that pattern, and I am determined that nobody shall find it out but myself!

Life is very much more exciting now than it used to be. You see I have something more to expect, to look forward to, to watch. I really do eat better, and am more quiet than I was.

John is so pleased to see me improve! He laughed a little the other day, and said I seemed to be flourishing in spite of my wallpaper.

I turned it off with a laugh. I had no intention of telling him it was *because* of the wallpaper—he would make fun of me. He might even want to take me away.

I don't want to leave now until I have found it out. There is a week more, and I think that will be enough.

I'm feeling ever so much better! I don't sleep much at night, for it is so interesting to watch developments; but I sleep a good deal in the daytime.

In the daytime it is tiresome and perplexing.

There are always new shoots on the fungus, and new shades of yellow all over it. I cannot keep count of them, though I have tried conscientiously.

It is the strangest yellow, that wallpaper! It makes me think of all the yellow things I ever saw—not beautiful ones like buttercups, but old foul, bad yellow things.

But there is something else about that paper—the smell! I noticed it the moment we came into the room, but with so much air and sun it was not bad. Now we have had a week of fog and rain, and whether the windows are open or not, the smell is here.

It creeps all over the house.

I find it hovering in the dining-room, skulking in the parlor, hiding in the hall, lying in wait for me on the stairs.

It gets into my hair.

Even when I go to ride, if I turn my head suddenly and surprise it— there is that smell!

Such a peculiar odor, too! I have spent hours in trying to analyze it, to find what it smelled like.

It is not bad—at first, and very gentle, but quite the subtlest, most enduring odor I ever met.

In this damp weather it is awful, I wake up in the night and find it hanging over me.

It used to disturb me at first. I thought seriously of burning the house—to reach the smell.

But now I am used to it. The only thing I can think of that it is like is the *color* of the paper! A yellow smell.

There is a very funny mark on this wall, low down, near the mop-board. A streak that runs round the room. It goes behind every piece of furniture, except the bed, a long, straight, even *smooch*, as if it had been rubbed over and over.

I wonder how it was done and who did it, and what they did it for. Round and round and round—round and round and round—it makes me dizzy!

I really have discovered something at last.

Through watching so much at night, when it changes so, I have finally found out.

The front pattern *does* move—and no wonder! The woman behind shakes it!

Sometimes I think there are a great many women behind, and sometimes only one, and she crawls around fast, and her crawling shakes it all over.

Then in the very bright spots she keeps still, and in the very shady spots she just takes hold of the bars and shakes them hard.

And she is all the time trying to climb through. But nobody could climb through that pattern—it strangles so; I think that is why it has so many heads.

They get through, and then the pattern strangles them off and turns them upside down, and makes their eyes white!

If those heads were covered or taken off it would not be half so bad.

I think that woman gets out in the daytime!

And I'll tell you why—privately—I've seen her!

I can see her out of every one of my windows!

It is the same woman, I know, for she is always creeping, and most women do not creep by daylight.

I see her in that long shaded lane, creeping up and down. I see her in those dark grape arbors, creeping all around the garden.

I see her on that long road under the trees, creeping along, and when a carriage comes she hides under the blackberry vines.

I don't blame her a bit. It must be very humiliating to be caught creeping by daylight!

I always lock the door when I creep by daylight. I can't do it at night, for I know John would suspect something at once.

And John is so queer now, that I don't want to irritate him. I wish he would take another room! Besides, I don't want anybody to get that woman out at night but myself.

I often wonder if I could see her out of all the windows at once.

But, turn as fast as I can, I can only see out of one at one time.

And though I always see her, she *may* be able to creep faster than I can turn!

I have watched her sometimes away off in the open country, creeping as fast as a cloud shadow in a high wind.

If only that top pattern could be gotten off from the under one! I mean to try it, little by little.

I have found out another funny thing, but I shan't tell it this time! It does not do to trust people too much.

There are only two more days to get this paper off, and I believe John is beginning to notice. I don't like the look in his eyes.

And I heard him ask Jennie a lot of professional questions, about me. She had a very good report to give.

She said I slept a good deal in the daytime.

John knows I don't sleep very well at night, for all I'm so quiet!

He asked me all sorts of questions too, and pretended to be very loving and kind.

As if I couldn't see through him!

Still, I don't wonder he acts so, sleeping under this paper for three months.

It only interests me, but I feel sure John and Jennie are secretly affected by it.

Hurrah! This is the last day, but it is enough. John to stay in town over night, and won't be out until this evening.

Jennie wanted to sleep with me—the sly thing! But I told her I should undoubtedly rest better for a night all alone.

That was clever, for really I wasn't alone a bit! As soon as it was moonlight and that poor thing began to crawl and shake the pattern, I got up and ran to help her.

I pulled and she shook, I shook and she pulled, and before morning we had peeled off yards of that paper.

A strip about as high as my head and half around the room.

And then when the sun came and that awful pattern began to laugh at me, I declared I would finish it to-day!

We go away to-morrow, and they are moving all my furniture down again to leave things as they were before.

Jennie looked at the wall in amazement, but I told her merrily that I did it out of pure spite at the vicious thing.

She laughed and said she wouldn't mind doing it herself, but I must not get tired.

How she betrayed herself that time!

But I am here, and no person touches this paper but me,—not *alive!*

She tried to get me out of the room—it was too patent! But I said it was so quiet and empty and clean now that I believed I would lie down again and sleep all I could, and not to wake me even for dinner—I would call when I woke.

So now she is gone, and the servants are gone, and the things are gone, and there is nothing left but that great bedstead nailed down, with the canvas mattress we found on it.

We shall sleep downstairs to-night, and take the boat home to-morrow.

I quite enjoy the room, now it is bare again.

How those children did tear about here!

This bedstead is fairly gnawed!

But I must get to work.

I have locked the door and thrown the key down into the front path.

I don't want to go out, and I don't want to have anybody come in, till John comes.

I want to astonish him.

I've got a rope up here that even Jennie did not find. If that woman does get out, and tries to get away, I can tie her!

But I forgot I could not reach far without anything to stand on!

This bed will *not* move!

I tried to lift and push it until I was lame, and then I got so angry I bit off a little piece at one corner—but it hurt my teeth.

Then I peeled off all the paper I could reach standing on the floor. It sticks horribly and the pattern just enjoys it! All those strangled heads and bulbous eyes and waddling fungus growths just shriek with derision!

I am getting angry enough to do something desperate. To jump out of the window would be admirable exercise, but the bars are too strong even to try.

Besides I wouldn't do it. Of course not. I know well enough that a step like that is improper and might be misconstrued.

I don't like to *look* out of the windows even—there are so many of those creeping women, and they creep so fast.

I wonder if they all come out of that wallpaper as I did?

But I am securely fastened now by my well-hidden rope—you don't get *me* out in the road there!

I suppose I shall have to get back behind the pattern when it comes night, and that is hard!

It is so pleasant to be out in this great room and creep around as I please!

I don't want to go outside. I won't, even if Jennie asks me to.

For outside you have to creep on the ground, and everything is green instead of yellow.

But here I can creep smoothly on the floor, and my shoulder just fits in that long smooch around the wall, so I cannot lose my way.

Why, there's John at the door!

It is no use, young man, you can't open it!

How he does call and pound!

Now he's crying for an axe.

It would be a shame to break down that beautiful door!

"John dear!" said I in the gentlest voice, "the key is down by the front steps, under a plantain leaf!"

That silenced him for a few moments.

Then he said—very quietly indeed, "Open the door, my darling!"

"I can't," said I. "The key is down by the front door under a plantain leaf!"

And then I said it again, several times, very gently and slowly, and said it so often that he had to go and see, and he got it of course, and came in. He stopped short by the door.

"What is the matter?" he cried. "For God's sake, what are you doing!"

I kept on creeping just the same, but I looked at him over my shoulder.

"I've got out at last," said I, "in spite of you and Jane. And I've pulled off most of the paper, so you can't put me back!"

Now why should that man have fainted? But he did, and right across my path by the wall, so that I had to creep over him every time!

[1892]

QUESTIONS ON THE STORIES

☐ How would you summarize the **plot** of each story? What makes it difficult to do so?

☐ Who, in your opinion, are the most sympathetic **characters**? Which are the most **antagonistic**? What kinds of information do we learn about the emotional lives of these characters?

☐ What is the **point of view** of each story? How would you compare the effects of these choices? What are the advantages and disadvantages of each choice?

☐ How would you describe the **setting** of each story?

☐ How would you describe the **style** of writing in each story? Is the prose formal? Archaic? Conversational? Melodramatic? Be as specific as possible, and note examples that bolster your claims.

☐ What kinds of **symbols** recur in each story? Are they fanciful? Ordinary? Conventional? Surprising? How do they move the narrative forward?

SAMPLE PAPER: AN ESSAY THAT COMPARES AND CONTRASTS

Melanie Smith was given the assignment to compare and contrast an element of her choosing in Chopin's "The Story of an Hour" and Gilman's "The Yellow Wallpaper," and to draw some conclusions about gender roles in the nineteenth century. Rather than examining the female protagonists,

Melanie chose to focus on the minor male characters in the stories. She wrote a point-by-point comparison designed to demonstrate that these men, despite the opinions of them that she heard expressed in class, were not bad people. Rather, they were led by their social training to behave in ways that were perfectly acceptable in their day, even if they now strike readers as oppressive.

Melanie Smith

English 109

Professor Hallet

18 May 2008

Good Husbands in Bad Marriages

When twenty-first-century readers first encounter literature of earlier times, it is easy for us to apply our own standards of conduct to the characters and situations. Kate Chopin's "The Story of an Hour" and Charlotte Perkins Gilman's "The Yellow Wallpaper" offer two good examples of this. Both written by American women in the last decade of the nineteenth century, the stories give us a look into the lives, and especially the marriages, of middle-class women of the time. By modern standards, the husbands of the two protagonists, particularly John in "The Yellow Wallpaper," seem almost unbearably controlling of their wives. From the vantage point of the late nineteenth century, however, their behavior looks quite different. Both men are essentially well meaning and try to be good husbands. Their only real crime is that they adhere too closely to the conventional Victorian wisdom about marriage.

Melanie signals that she will focus on these two stories and makes a claim about them that she will go on to support.

To begin with, both men are well respected in their communities. John in "The Yellow Wallpaper" is described as "a physician of high standing" who has "an intense horror of superstition, and he scoffs openly at any talk of things not to be felt and seen and put down in figures." These are just the qualities that we might expect to find in a respectable doctor, even today. It is less clear what Brently Mallard in "The Story of an Hour" does for a living. (In fact, Chopin's story is so short that we learn fairly little about any of the characters.) But the couple seems to live in a comfortable house, and they are surrounded by family and friends, suggesting a secure, well-connected lifestyle. In the nineteenth century, a man's most important job was to

Melanie's first observation about what the male characters have in common.

take care of his wife and family, and both men in these stories seem to be performing this job very well.

In addition to providing a comfortable life for them, it also seems that both men love their wives. When she believes her husband has died, Mrs. Mallard thinks of his "kind, tender hands folded in death; the face that had never looked save with love upon her." Her own love for him is less certain, which may be why she feels "free" when he dies, but his for her seems genuine. The case of John in "The Yellow Wallpaper" is a bit more compli- cated. To a modern reader, it seems that he treats his wife more like a child than a grown woman. He puts serious restraints on her actions, and at one point he even calls her "little girl." But he also calls her "my darling" and "dear," and she does say, "He loves me very dearly." When he has to leave her alone, he even has his sister come to look after her, which is a kind gesture, even if it seems a bit like he doesn't trust his wife. If the narrator, who is in a position to know, doesn't doubt her husband's love, what gives us the right to judge it?

To a certain extent, we must admit that both husbands do oppress their wives by being overprotective. Part of the point of both stories is to show how even acceptable, supposedly good marriages of the day could be overly confining to women. This is especially obvious when we see how much John restricts his wife — forbidding her even to visit her cousins or to write letters — and how everyone expects her to agree to his demands. Though Mrs. Mallard isn't literally confined to a house or a room the way the narrator of "The Yellow Wallpaper" is, she stays inside the house and is looking out the window longingly when she realizes she wants to be free. But it is important for a reader not to blame the husbands, because they really don't intend to be oppressive.

In fact, it is true that both of the wives are in somewhat frail health. Mrs. Mallard is "afflicted with a heart trouble," and the narrator of "The Yellow Wallpaper" seems to have many

A smooth tra tion into the point.

Melanie es lishes a si between th husbands

A point similar between wives.

physical and mental problems, so it is not surprising that their husbands worry about them. It is not evil intent that leads the men to act as they do, it is simply ignorance. John seems less innocent then Brently because he is so patronizing and he puts such restrictions on his wife's behavior and movement, but that kind of attitude was normal for the day, and as a doctor, John seems really to be doing what he thinks is best.

All the other characters in the stories see both men as good and loving husbands, which suggests that society would have approved of their behavior. Even the wives themselves, who are the victims of these oppressive marriages, don't blame the men at all. The narrator of "The Yellow Wallpaper" even thinks she is "ungrateful" when she doesn't appreciate John's loving care more. Once we understand this, readers should not be too quick to blame the men either. The real blame falls to the society that gave these men the idea that women are frail and need protection from the world. The men may be the immediate cause of the women's suffering, but the real cause is much deeper and has to do with cultural attitudes and how the men were brought up to protect and provide for women.

Melanie returns to her original claim.

Most people who live in a society don't see the flaws in that society's conventional ways of thinking and living. We now know that women are capable and independent and that protecting them as if they were children ultimately does more harm than good. But in the late Victorian era, such an idea would have seemed either silly or dangerously radical to most people, men and women alike. Stories like these, however, could have helped their original readers begin to think about how confining these supposedly good marriages were. Fortunately, authors such as Chopin and Gilman come along from time to time and show us the problems in our conventional thinking, so society can move forward and we can begin to see how even the most well-meaning actions should sometimes be questioned.

Melanie's conclusion argues for the idea that literature is capable of challenging the status quo.

CHAPTER 5

Writing about Poems

As with stories, there are certain elements you should be aware of as you prepare to write about poetry. Sometimes these elements are the same as for fiction. A **narrative poem**, for instance, will have a **plot**, **setting**, and **characters**, and all poems speak from a particular point of view. To the extent that any of the elements of fiction help you to understand a poem, by all means use them in your analysis. Poetry, however, does present a special set of concerns for a reader, and elements of poetry frequently provide rich ground for analysis.

ELEMENTS OF POETRY

The Speaker

First, consider the speaker of the poem. Imagine that someone is saying the words of this poem aloud. Who is speaking, where is this **speaker**, and what is his or her state of mind? Sometimes the voice is that of the poet him- or herself, but frequently a poem speaks from a different perspective, just as a short story might be from a point of view very different from the author's. It's not always apparent when this is the case, but some poets will signal who the speaker is in a title, as Christopher Marlowe does in "The Passionate Shepherd to His Love" or T. S. Eliot in "The Love Song of J. Alfred Prufrock." Be alert to signals that will help you recognize the speaker, and remember that some poems have more than one speaker.

The Listener

Be attentive also to any other persons in the poem, particularly an **implied listener**. Is there a "you" to whom the poem is addressed? If the poem is being spoken aloud, who is supposed to hear it? When, early in his poem "Dover Beach," Matthew Arnold writes, "Come to the window, sweet is the night-air!" he gives us an important clue as to how to read the poem. We should imagine both the speaker and the implied listener together in a room, with a window open to the night. As we read on, we can look for further clues as to who these two people are and why they are together on this night. Many poems create a relationship between the "I" of the speaker and the "you" of the listener; however, that is not always the case. Sometimes the speaker does not address a "you" and instead provides a more philosophical meditation that isn't explicitly addressed to a listener. Consider the effect of these poems: Do they feel more abstract? More detached from the material conditions of time and place? Do they provide certainty, or resolution? The questions about the speaker and listener are crucial to your analysis of poetry.

Imagery

Just as you should be open to the idea that there are frequently symbols in stories, you should pay special attention to the **images** in poems. Although poems are often about such grand themes as love or death, they rarely dwell long in these abstractions. Rather, the best poetry seeks to make the abstraction concrete by creating vivid images appealing directly to the senses. A well-written poem will provide the mind of an attentive reader with sights, sounds, tastes, scents, and sensations. Since poems tend to be short and densely packed with meaning, every word and image is there for a reason. Isolate these images and give some thought to what they make you think and how they make you feel. Are they typical or unexpected?

Consider these lines from John Donne's "The Good Morrow":

> My face in thine eye, thine in mine appears,
> And true plain hearts do in the faces rest;
> Where can we find two better hemispheres,
> Without sharp north, without declining west? (lines 15–18)

Here, Donne celebrates the love between the speaker and his object of desire, comparing the faces of the lovers to two "hemispheres" on globes. Elsewhere in the poem, Donne uses imagery that is borrowed from the world of navigation and mapping; here, he suggests that the lovers' faces are an improvement upon whatever instruments explorers and learned men use to understand the world. By examining the images in a poem, their placement, juxtaposition, and effect, you will have gone a long way toward understanding the poem as a whole.

Sound and Sense

Of all the genres, poetry is the one that most self-consciously highlights **language**, so it is necessary to pay special attention to the sounds of a poem. In fact, it is always a good idea to read a poem aloud several times, giving yourself the opportunity to experience the role that sound plays in the poem's meaning.

Patterns of Sound

Much of the poetry written in English before the twentieth century was written in some form of **rhyme**, and contemporary poets continue to experiment with its effects. Rhymes may seem stilted or old-fashioned to our twenty-first-century ears, but keep in mind that rhymes have powerful social meanings in the cultural context in which they're written.

End-Rhymes

Here is just one example of an **end-rhyme** (rhymes that appear at the ends of lines in a poem). Let's look at a **heroic couplet** from Robert Browning's "My Last Duchess":

> Sir, 'twas all one! My favor at her breast,
> The dropping of the daylight in the West, (lines 25-26)

Here, Browning rhymes "breast" with "West," and in doing so equates them as part of a comparison. As you read poems, ask yourself how pairs of rhymes work. Do they create **juxtapositions**? Alignments of meaning? And what is the effect of that relationship as the poem progresses?

Assonance and Consonance

While it is important to look at the end of a line to see how the poet uses sounds, it is also important to look inside the line. Poets use **assonance** to create an aural effect among vowel sounds. Consider these opening lines from Gerard Manley Hopkins's "Pied Beauty":

> Glory be to God for dappled things —
>   For skies of couple-colour as a brinded cow;
>   For rose-moles all in stipple upon trout that swim;
> Fresh-firecoal chestnut-falls; finches' wings;
>   Landscape plotted and pieced — fold, fallow, and plough;
>   And all trades, their gear and tackle and trim. (lines 1-6)

Throughout these lines, Hopkins pays special attention to "uh" and "ow" sounds. Notice "couple-colour" and "cow" in line 2, "upon" and "trout" in line 3, "fallow" and "plough" in line 5. As you read through each line ask yourself: Why does the poet align these sounds? Do these sounds speed up the tempo of the line, or slow it down? What do these sounds — and words — reveal about the poet's praise of "dappled things"?

Poets also use **consonance** to create alignments and juxtapositions among consonants. Consider these first lines from Christopher Marlowe's "The Passionate Shepherd to His Love":

> Come live with me and be my love,
> And we will all the pleasures prove (lines 1–2)

In line 1, Marlowe aligns "live" with "love" to suggest that there is an equation between cohabitation and romance. In line 2, he aligns the "p" sound in "pleasures prove"; in addition, though, the **slant rhyme** of "love" and "prove" also creates meaning between the lines. What "proof" is there in love? Is love what will make the speaker feel most alive?

Form

Poets writing in English use dozens of traditional forms from a variety of traditions. Some of the most common of these forms are the **sonnet**, the **villanelle**, the **sestina**, and the **ballad**, but there are too many to name here. As you read a poem in a traditional form, think of the form as a kind of template in which poets arrange and explore challenging emotional and intellectual material. A sonnet, for example, has a concise fourteen-line iambic pentameter structure that allows the poet to address a religious, romantic, or philosophical argument in a very compressed space. As you read a sonnet, you might ask yourself: What does its form accomplish that's different from, say, a ballad or **pantoum** or **triolet**?

Note, too, that many contemporary poets write in **free verse**, which means that they do not necessarily use a strict traditional form or meter for their poems. That doesn't mean that the free verse poet is writing without rules; it just means that the poet is creating his or her own system for the unique needs of each poem.

Meter

Poetry written in English is both **accentual** and **syllabic**. That is, poets count the number of accents as well as the number of syllables as they create each line of poetry. The most common meter in English poetry is **iambic pentameter**, which consists of five **accents** with two **syllables** in each accent. Consider the first four lines of John Donne's Holy Sonnet XIV ("Batter my heart"). Donne's lines are written in iambic pentameter, but have a lot of variation, too. As you read, notice where Donne places the emphasis in each line:

> **Bat**ter my **heart**, three-**per**soned God, for **you**
> As **yet** but **knock**, **breathe**, **shine**, and **seek** to **mend**;
> That **I** may **rise** and **stand**, o'er**throw** me, and **bend**
> Your **force** to **break**, **blow**, **burn**, and **make** me **new**. (lines 1–4)

Note that not every line is a perfect iamb; in line 1, Donne starts with an accent on the first syllable instead of the second one, disrupting the unstressed/stressed beat of the iambic line. Then, in line 2, Donne uses three strong monosyllabic words in a row to mimic the kind of aggression that the speaker requests from God. Donne does this again in line 4, with "break, blow, burn," which mirrors the sounds and sense of line 2. Donne continually disrupts the flow of iambic pentameter in order to reveal the difficulty of his spiritual struggle.

Iambic pentameter is only one of many kinds of meter in English, and each meter has its own unique properties and effects. When you read a poem, listen to each line to find out how many accents and syllables it contains, then determine what that meter is and how the poet uses— and subverts—that formula as part of a strategy for the poem.

Stanzas

A **stanza** is any grouping of lines of poetry into a unit. The word *stanza* comes from the Italian for "room." As you read poetry, imagine each stanza as a room with its own correspondences and relationships, and consider how that stanza creates a singular effect. Sometimes a stanza can be one line long; sometimes the poet creates a block of lines with no stanza breaks. All of these choices create distinct effects for readers of poetry.

Lineation

Lineation—or how a poet uses the lines in the poem—is a crucial component of poetry. Sometimes poets use punctuation at the end of every line, but more often they mix end-stopped lines with enjambed lines. **Enjambment** occurs when the line is not end-stopped with a comma, dash, or period. Its meaning spills over onto the next line, creating the effect of acceleration and intensity. Poets also use **caesuras** in the middle of lines to create variety in the pattern of the line. A caesura is a deep pause created by a comma, colon, semicolon, dash, period, or white space. Consider the use of enjambment and caesura in this excerpt from Browning's "My Last Duchess":

Or blush, at least. She thanked men, — good! but thanked
Somehow — I know not how — as if she ranked
My gift of a nine-hundred-years-old name
With anybody's gift. Who'd stoop to blame
This sort of trifling? Even had you skill (lines 31–35)

Look at the way Browning breaks up the monotony of the iambic pentameter in this excerpt. He uses enjambment at the end of each line, forcing the reader to move quickly through the line break to catch the rest of the sentence's meaning in the following line. The long dashes followed by "good!" and "I know not how" create a sense of remove between what the speaker wants us to know versus what's going on inside his head. Browning creates deep pauses, or caesuras, in lines 31 and 34 by ending one sentence and beginning a new one in the middle of the line. With these variations, Browning enlivens his lines with cues for a more dramatic performance of the poem.

There are many kinds of rhyme schemes, forms, and meters for poetry written in English. For more information, see the "Elements of Poetry" online tutorial at: http://bcs.bedfordstmartins.com/virtualit/poetry/rhyme_def.html

A POEM FOR ANALYSIS

Take a few minutes to read William Shakespeare's Sonnet 116 and consider the questions about it on page 88. Although the poem is brief, it is complex. What elements of poetry do you notice in it?

WILLIAM SHAKESPEARE   [1564–1616]

Sonnet 116

Let me not to the marriage of true minds
Admit impediments. Love is not love
Which alters when it alteration finds,
Or bends with the remover to remove.
O, no, it is an ever-fixèd mark   5
That looks on tempests and is never shaken;

It is the star to every wandering bark,°   *ship*
Whose worth's unknown, although his height be taken.°   *is measured*
Love's not time's fool, though rosy lips and cheeks
Within his bending sickle's compass come;   10
Love alters not with his brief hours and weeks,
But bears it out even to the edge of doom.°   *Judgment Day*
    If this be error and upon me proved,
    I never writ, nor no man ever loved.

                                                                                        [1609]

QUESTIONS ON THE POEM

☐ What **images** are most striking in this poem? Do they seem
   conventional, surprising, experimental? Why?

☐ A **sonnet** often reveals its own logic in order to argue for a
   point of view. What is the argument of this poem? Do you find
   it persuasive? If not, why not?

☐ What is the **rhyme** structure of this sonnet? What words are
   aligned as a result of this scheme?

☐ How does Shakespeare use **enjambment** and **caesura** to
   manage the tempo of the poem? What effects does this create?

SAMPLE PAPER: AN EXPLICATION

Patrick McCorkle, the author of the paper that follows, was given the
assignment to perform a close reading of one of Shakespeare's sonnets.
He needed first to pick a poem and then to choose specific features of its
language to isolate and analyze. He chose Shakespeare's Sonnet 116
because it seemed to him to offer an interesting and balanced definition
of love. After rereading the poem, he became interested in several unex-
pectedly negative, even unsettling images that seemed out of place in a
poem about the positive emotion of love. This was a good start, and it
allowed him to write a draft of the paper. When he was finished, however, the essay was a little shorter than he had hoped it would be. During
a peer workshop in class, he discussed the sonnet and his draft with two
classmates, and together they noticed how many negative words appeared in the poem as well. That was the insight Patrick needed to fill
out his essay and feel satisfied with the results.

Patrick McCorkle

Professor Bobrick

English 102

10 January 2008

Shakespeare Defines Love

From the earliest written rhymes to the latest top-40 radio hit, love is among the eternal themes for poetry. Most love poetry seems to fall into one of two categories. Either the poet sings the praises of the beloved and the unending joys of love in overly exaggerated terms, or the poet laments the loss of love with such bitterness and distress that it seems like the end of life. Anyone who has been in love, though, can tell you that both of these views are limited and incomplete and that real love is neither entirely joyous nor entirely sad. In Sonnet 116, "Let me not to the marriage of true minds," Shakespeare creates a more realistic image of love. By balancing negative with positive images and language, this sonnet does a far better job than thousands of songs and poems before and since, defining love in all its complexities and contradictions.

Patrick identifies his topic and states his thesis.

Like many poems, Sonnet 116 relies on a series of visual images to paint vivid pictures for a reader, but not all of these images are what we might expect in a poem celebrating the pleasures of lasting love. A reader can easily picture "an ever-fixèd mark," a "tempest," a "star," a "wandering bark" (meaning a boat lost at sea), "rosy lips and cheeks," and a "bending sickle." Some of these, like stars and rosy lips, are just the sort of sunny, positive images we typically find in love poems of the joyous variety. Others, though, are more unexpected. Flowers and images of springtime, for instance, are standard issue in happy love poetry, but a sickle is associated with autumn and the death of the year, and metaphorically with death itself in the form of the grim reaper. Likewise, a boat tossed in a raging tempest is not exactly the typical poetic depiction of happy love.

Patrick introduces the poem's contradictory imagery.

Such pictures would hardly seem to provide an upbeat image of what love is all about, and in fact they might be more at home in one of the sad poems about the loss of love. But these tempests and sickles are more realistic than the hearts and flowers of so many lesser love poems. In fact, they show that the poet recognizes the bad times that occur in all relationships, even those strong enough to inspire love sonnets. And the negative images are tempered because of the contexts in which they occur. The "wandering bark" for instance might represent trouble and loss, but love itself is seen as the star that will lead the boat safely back to calm waters. Meanwhile, the beloved's "rosy lips and cheeks" may fade, but real love outlives even the stroke of death's sickle, lasting "to the edge of doom."

Patrick expl⟨
the effect of
imagery.

Just as positive and negative images are juxtaposed, so are positive and negative language. The first four lines of Sonnet 116 are made up of two sentences, both negatives, beginning with the words "Let me not" and "Love is not." The negatives of the first few lines continue in phrases like "Whose worth's unknown" and "Love's not time's fool." From here, the poem goes on to dwell in abstract ideas such as "alteration," "impediments," and "error." None of this is what readers of love poems have been led to expect in their previous reading, and we might even wonder if the poet finds this love thing worth the trouble. This strange and unexpected language continues on through the last line of the poem, which contains no fewer than three negative words: "never," "nor," and "no."

Patrick int
direct quo⟨
from the p⟨
into his cl⟨
reading.

Where, a reader might ask, are the expected positive descriptions of love? Where are the summer skies, the smiles and laughter? Clearly, Shakespeare doesn't mean to sweep his readers up in rosy images of a lover's bliss. Ultimately, though, even with the preponderance of negative images and words, the poem strikes a hopeful tone. The hedging about what love isn't and what it can't do are balanced with positive words and phrases, saying clearly what love is: "it is an ever-fixèd mark" and "it is the star." Love, it would seem, does not make our lives perfect, but it gives us the strength, stability, and direction to survive the bad times.

Though more than 400 years have passed since Shakespeare wrote his sonnets, some things never change, and among these is the nature of complex human emotions. In a mere fourteen lines, Shakespeare succeeds where many others have failed through the years, providing a much more satisfying definition of love than one normally sees in one-dimensional, strictly happy or sad poetry. The love he describes is the sort that not everyone is lucky enough to find — a "marriage of true minds" — complicated, unsettling, and very real.

In his conclusion, Patrick suggests that the poem is successful because of the juxtapositions he has discussed.

CHAPTER 6

Writing about Plays

Perhaps the earliest literary critic in the Western tradition was Aristotle, who, in the fifth century B.C.E., set about explaining the power of the genre of **tragedy** by identifying the six **elements of drama** and analyzing the contribution each of these elements makes to the functioning of a play as a whole. The elements Aristotle identified as common to all dramas were plot, characterization, theme, diction, melody, and spectacle. Some of these are the same as or very similar to the basic components of prose fiction and poetry, but others are slightly different when it comes to drama.

ELEMENTS OF DRAMA

The words *plot*, *character*, and *theme* mean basically the same thing in drama as they do in fiction, though there is a difference in how they are presented. A story *tells* you about a series of events, whereas a play *shows* you these events happening in real time. The information that might be conveyed in descriptive passages in prose fiction must be conveyed in a play through **dialogue** (and to a lesser extent through **stage directions** and the **set** and character descriptions that sometimes occur at the start of a play). This means that as a reader you must be especially attentive to nuances of language in a play, which often means imagining what might be happening onstage during a particular passage of speech. Using your imagination in this way—in effect, staging the play in your mind—will help you with some of the difficulties inherent in play reading. If you have access to film versions of the play that you will examine, be sure to watch them. Drama is a living art, and if you read the play text on the page, you are only getting one part of what has made drama so important to all cultures across many time periods. If you are reading a Shakespeare play, you can be certain that there are several film versions to choose from, many of which might be in your library's collection. Check your local theater listings to see what they are staging; you might find that a theater company is performing the play that you have to read for your class.

When Aristotle speaks of **diction**, he means the specific words that a playwright chooses to put into the mouth of a character. In a well-written play, different characters will have different ways of speaking, and these will tell us a good deal about their character and personality. Does one character sound very formal and well educated? Does another speak in slang or dialect? Does someone hesitate or speak in fits and starts, perhaps indicating distraction or nervousness? Practice paying attention to these nuances. And keep in mind that just because a character says something, that doesn't make it true. As in real life, some characters might be hiding the truth or even telling outright lies.

When Aristotle writes of melody, he is referring to the fact that Greek drama was written in verse and was chanted or sung onstage. The role of **melody** shifts with the work created in different cultures and time periods. In the English Renaissance, Shakespeare and his contemporaries used iambic pentameter and occasional end-rhymes to create dramas in verse, and staged productions have always used some kind of music, whether it be instrumental, vocal, or a mix of both. Melody is much less significant in drama today, though some plays do contain songs, of course, and the rhythm of spoken words can be important in a play, just as it is in a poem. **Spectacle** refers to what we actually see onstage when we go to a play—the costumes, the actors' movements, the sets, the lights, and so forth. In reading a play, it is important to remember that it was not written to be read only, but rather so that it would be seen onstage in the communal setting of a theater. Reading with this in mind and trying to imagine the spectacle of a real production will increase your enjoyment of plays immensely.

Setting, which Aristotle ignores completely, is just as important in drama as it is in fiction. But again, in drama it must be either displayed onstage or alluded to through the characters' words rather than being described as it might in a story or a poem. Modern plays often (though not always) begin with elaborate descriptions of the stage, furniture, major props, and so forth, which can be very useful in helping you to picture a production. These tend to be absent in older plays, so in some cases you will have to use your imagination. In Act 4 of *Hamlet*, the characters are in a castle one moment and on a windswept plain the next. The words and actions of characters at times sufficiently signal a change of locale.

A PLAY FOR ANALYSIS

Trifles, the one-act play by Susan Glaspell that follows, is on one level a murder mystery and on another a critique of and commentary on gender roles and stereotypes. The questions after the play ask you to consider how the elements of drama contribute to its effects and impact.

SUSAN GLASPELL [1882–1948]

Trifles

Characters
GEORGE HENDERSON, *county attorney*
HENRY PETERS, *sheriff*
LEWIS HALE, *a neighboring farmer*
MRS. PETERS
MRS. HALE

Scene: *The kitchen in the now abandoned farmhouse of John Wright, a gloomy kitchen, and left without having been put in order—the walls covered with a faded wall paper. Down right is a door leading to the parlor. On the right wall above this door is a built-in kitchen cupboard with shelves in the upper portion and drawers below. In the rear wall at right, up two steps is a door opening onto stairs leading to the second floor. In the rear wall at left is a door to the shed and from there to the outside. Between these two doors is an old-fashioned black iron stove. Running along the left wall from the shed door is an old iron sink and sink shelf, in which is set a hand pump. Downstage of the sink is an uncurtained window. Near the window is an old wooden rocker. Center stage is an unpainted wooden kitchen table with straight chairs on either side. There is a small chair down right. Unwashed pans under the sink, a loaf of bread outside the breadbox, a dish towel on the table— other signs of incompleted work. At the rear the shed door opens and the Sheriff comes in followed by the County Attorney and Hale. The Sheriff and Hale are men in middle life, the County Attorney is a young man; all are much bundled up and go at once to the stove. They are followed by the two women—the Sheriff's wife, Mrs. Peters, first: she is a slight wiry woman, a thin nervous face. Mrs. Hale is larger and would ordinarily be called more comfortable looking, but she is disturbed now and looks fearfully about as she enters. The women have come in slowly, and stand close together near the door.*

COUNTY ATTORNEY (*at stove rubbing his hands*): This feels good. Come up to the fire, ladies.

MRS. PETERS (*after taking a step forward*): I'm not—cold.

SHERIFF (*unbuttoning his overcoat and stepping away from the stove to right of table as if to mark the beginning of official business*): Now, Mr. Hale, before we move things about, you explain to Mr. Henderson just what you saw when you came here yesterday morning.

COUNTY ATTORNEY (*crossing down to left of the table*): By the way, has anything been moved? Are things just as you left them yesterday?

94

SHERIFF (*looking about*): It's just about the same. When it dropped below zero last night I thought I'd better send Frank out this morning to make a fire for us—(*sits right of center table*) no use getting pneumonia with a big case on, but I told him not to touch anything except the stove—and you know Frank.

COUNTY ATTORNEY: Somebody should have been left here yesterday.

SHERIFF: Oh—yesterday. When I had to send Frank to Morris Center for that man who went crazy—I want you to know I had my hands full yesterday. I knew you could get back from Omaha by today and as long as I went over everything here myself———

COUNTY ATTORNEY: Well, Mr. Hale, tell just what happened when you came here yesterday morning.

HALE (*crossing down to above table*): Harry and I had started to town with a load of potatoes. We came along the road from my place and as I got here I said, "I'm going to see if I can't get John Wright to go in with me on a party telephone." I spoke to Wright about it once before and he put me off, saying folks talked too much anyway, and all he asked was peace and quiet—I guess you know about how much he talked himself; but I thought maybe if I went to the house and talked about it before his wife, though I said to Harry that I didn't know as what his wife wanted made much difference to John———

COUNTY ATTORNEY: Let's talk about that later, Mr. Hale. I do want to talk about that, but tell now just what happened when you got to the house.

HALE: I didn't hear or see anything; I knocked at the door, and still it was all quiet inside. I knew they must be up, it was past eight o'clock. So I knocked again, and I thought I heard someone say, "Come in." I wasn't sure, I'm not sure yet, but I opened the door—this door (*indicating the door by which the two women are still standing*) and there in that rocker—(*pointing to it*) sat Mrs. Wright. (*They all look at the rocker down left.*)

COUNTY ATTORNEY: What—was she doing?

HALE: She was rockin' back and forth. She had her apron in her hand and was kind of—pleating it.

COUNTY ATTORNEY: And how did she—look?

HALE: Well, she looked queer.

COUNTY ATTORNEY: How do you mean—queer?

HALE: Well, as if she didn't know what she was going to do next. And kind of done up.

COUNTY ATTORNEY (*takes out notebook and pencil and sits left of center table*): How did she seem to feel about your coming?

HALE: Why, I don't think she minded—one way or other. She didn't pay much attention. I said, "How do, Mrs. Wright, it's cold, ain't it?" And she said, "Is it?"—and went on kind of pleating at her apron. Well, I was surprised: she didn't ask me to come up to the stove, or to set down, but just sat there, not even looking at me, so I said, "I want to see John." And then she—laughed. I guess you would call it a laugh. I thought of Harry and the team outside, so I said a little sharp: "Can't I see John?" "No," she says, kind o' dull like. "Ain't he home?" says I. "Yes," says she, "he's home." "Then why can't I see him?" I asked her, out of patience. "'Cause he's dead," says she. "*Dead?*" says I. She just nodded her head, not getting a bit excited, but rockin' back and forth. "Why—where is he?" says I, not knowing what to say. She just pointed upstairs—like that. (*Himself pointing to the room above.*) I started for the stairs, with the idea of going up there. I walked from there to here—then I says, "Why, what did he die of?" "He died of a rope round his neck," says she, and just went on pleatin' at her apron. Well, I went out and called Harry. I thought I might—need help. We went upstairs and there he was lyin'———

COUNTY ATTORNEY: I think I'd rather have you go into that upstairs, where you can point it all out. Just go on now with the rest of the story.

HALE: Well, my first thought was to get that rope off. It looked . . . (*stops: his face twitches*) . . . but Harry, he went up to him, and he said, "No, he's dead all right, and we'd better not touch anything." So we went right back downstairs. She was still sitting that same way. "Has anybody been notified?" I asked. "No," says she, unconcerned. "Who did this, Mrs. Wright?" said Harry. He said it businesslike—and she stopped pleatin' of her apron. "I don't know," she says. "You don't *know?*" says Harry. "No," says she. "Weren't you sleepin' in the bed with him?" says Harry. "Yes," says she, "but I was on the inside." "Somebody slipped a rope round his head and strangled him and you didn't wake up?" says Harry. "I didn't wake up," she said after him. We must 'a' looked as if we didn't see how that could be, for after a minute she said, "I sleep sound." Harry was going to ask her more questions but I said maybe we ought to let her tell her story first to the coroner, or the sheriff, so Harry went fast as he could to Rivers' place, where there's a telephone.

COUNTY ATTORNEY: And what did Mrs. Wright do when she knew that you had gone for the coroner?

HALE: She moved from the rocker to that chair over there (*pointing to a small chair in the down right corner*) and just sat there with her hands held together and looking down. I got a feeling that I ought to make some conversation, so I said I had come in to see if John wanted to put in a telephone, and at that she started to laugh, and then she stopped and looked at me—scared. (*The County Attorney, who has ha his notebook out, makes a note.*) I dunno, maybe it wasn't scared. I wouldn't like to say it was. Soon Harry got back, and then Dr. Lloyd came and you, Mr. Peters, and so I guess that's all I know that you don't.

COUNTY ATTORNEY (*rising and looking around*): I guess we'll go upstairs first—and then out to the barn and around there. (*To the Sheriff.*) You're convinced that there was nothing important here—nothing that would point to any motive?

SHERIFF: Nothing here but kitchen things. (*The County Attorney, after again looking around the kitchen, opens the door of a cupboard closet in right wall. He brings a small chair from right—gets on it and looks on a shelf. Pulls his hand away, sticky.*)

COUNTY ATTORNEY: Here's a nice mess. (*The women draw nearer up to center.*)

MRS. PETERS (*to the other woman*): Oh, her fruit; it did freeze. (*To the Lawyer.*) She worried about that when it turned so cold. She said the fire'd go out and her jars would break.

SHERIFF (*rises*): Well, can you beat the woman! Held for murder and worryin' about her preserves.

COUNTY ATTORNEY (*getting down from chair*): I guess before we're through she may have something more serious than preserves to worry about. (*Crosses down right center.*)

HALE: Well, women are used to worrying over trifles. (*The two women move a little closer together.*)

COUNTY ATTORNEY (*with the gallantry of a young politician*): And yet, for all their worries, what would we do without the ladies? (*The women do not unbend. He goes below the center table to the sink, takes a dipperful of water from the pail, and pouring it into a basin, washes his hands. While he is doing this the Sheriff and Hale cross to cupboard, which they inspect. The County Attorney starts to wipe his hands on the roller towel, turns it for a cleaner place.*) Dirty towels! (*Kicks his foot against the pans under the sink.*) Not much of a housekeeper, would you say, ladies?

MRS. HALE (*stiffly*): There's a great deal of work to be done on a farm.

COUNTY ATTORNEY: To be sure. And yet (*with a little bow to her*) I know there are some Dickson County farmhouses which do not have such roller towels. (*He gives it a pull to expose its full-length again.*)

MRS. HALE: Those towels get dirty awful quick. Men's hands aren't always clean as they might be.

COUNTY ATTORNEY: Ah, loyal to your sex, I see. But you and Mrs. Wright were neighbors. I suppose you were friends, too.

MRS. HALE (*shaking her head*): I've not seen much of her of late years. I've not been in this house—it's more than a year.

COUNTY ATTORNEY (*crossing to women up center*): And why was that? You didn't like her?

MRS. HALE: I liked her all well enough. Farmer's wives have their hands full, Mr. Henderson. And then——

COUNTY ATTORNEY: Yes——?

MRS. HALE (*looking about*): It never seemed a very cheerful place.

COUNTY ATTORNEY: No—it's not cheerful. I shouldn't say she had the homemaking instinct.

MRS. HALE: Well, I don't know as Wright had, either.

COUNTY ATTORNEY: You mean that they didn't get on very well?

MRS. HALE: No, I don't mean anything. But I don't think a place'd be any cheerfuller for John Wright's being in it.

COUNTY ATTORNEY: I'd like to talk more of that a little later. I want to get the lay of things upstairs now. (*He goes past the women to up right where the steps lead to a stair door.*)

SHERIFF: I suppose anything Mrs. Peters does'll be all right. She was to take in some clothes for her, you know, and a few little things. We left in such a hurry yesterday.

COUNTY ATTORNEY: Yes, but I would like to see what you take, Mrs. Peters, and keep an eye out for anything that might be of use to us.

MRS. PETERS: Yes, Mr. Henderson. (*The men leave by up right door to stairs. The women listen to the men's steps on the stairs, then look about the kitchen.*)

MRS. HALE (*crossing left to sink*): I'd hate to have men coming into my kitchen, snooping around and criticizing. (*She arranges the pans under sink which the lawyer had shoved out of place.*)

MRS. PETERS: Of course it's no more than their duty. (*Crosses to cupboard up right.*)

MRS. HALE: Duty's all right, but I guess that deputy sheriff that came out to make the fire might have got a little of this on. (*Gives the roller towel a pull.*) Wish I'd thought of that sooner. Seems mean to talk about her for not having things slicked up when she had to come away in such a hurry. (*Crosses right to Mrs. Peters at cupboard.*)

MRS. PETERS (*who has been looking through cupboard, lifts one end of towel that covers a pan*): She had bread set. (*Stands still.*)

MRS. HALE (*eyes fixed on a loaf of bread beside the breadbox, which is on a low shelf of the cupboard*): She was going to put this in there. (*Picks up loaf, abruptly drops it. In a manner of returning to familiar things.*) It's a shame about her fruit. I wonder if it's all gone. (*Gets up on chair and looks.*) I think there's some here that's all right, Mrs. Peters. Yes— here; (*holding it toward the window*) this is cherries, too. (*Looking again.*) I declare I believe that's the only one. (*Gets down, jar in hand. Goes to the sink and wipes it off on the outside.*) She'll feel awfu bad after all her hard work in the hot weather. I remember the after-noon I put up my cherries last summer. (*She puts the jar on the big kitchen table, center of the room. With a sigh, is about to sit down in the rocking chair. Before she is seated realizes what chair it is; with a slow look at it, steps back. The chair which she has touched rocks back and forth. Mrs. Peters moves to center table and they both watch the chair rock for a moment or two.*)

MRS. PETERS (*shaking off the mood which the empty rocking chair has evoked. Now in a businesslike manner she speaks*): Well I must get those things from the front room closet. (*She goes to the door at the right but, after looking into the other room, steps back.*) You coming with me, Mrs. Hale? You could help me carry them. (*They go in the other room; reappear, Mrs. Peters carrying a dress, petticoat, and skirt, Mrs. Hale following with a pair of shoes.*) My, it's cold in there. (*She puts the clothes on the big table and hurries to the stove.*)

MRS. HALE (*right of center table examining the skirt*): Wright was close. I think maybe that's why she kept so much to herself. She didn't even belong to the Ladies' Aid. I suppose she felt she couldn't do her part, and then you don't enjoy things when you feel shabby. I heard she used to wear pretty clothes and be lively, when she was Minnie Foster, one of the town girls singing in the choir. But that—oh, that was thirty years ago. This all you want to take in?

MRS. PETERS: She said she wanted an apron. Funny thing to want, for there isn't much to get you dirty in jail, goodness knows. But I suppose just to make her feel more natural. (*Crosses to cupboard.*) She said they was in the top drawer in this cupboard. Yes, here. And then her little shawl that always hung behind the door. (*Opens stair door and looks.*) Yes, here it is. (*Quickly shuts door leading upstairs.*)

MRS. HALE (*abruptly moving toward her*): Mrs. Peters?

MRS. PETERS: Yes, Mrs. Hale? (*At up right door.*)

MRS. HALE: Do you think she did it?

MRS. PETERS (*in a frightened voice*): Oh, I don't know.

MRS. HALE: Well, I don't think she did. Asking for an apron and her little shawl. Worrying about her fruit.

MRS. PETERS (*starts to speak, glances up, where footsteps are heard in the room above. In a low voice*): Mr. Peters says it looks bad for her. Mr. Henderson is awful sarcastic in a speech and he'll make fun of her sayin' she didn't wake up.

MRS. HALE: Well, I guess John Wright didn't wake when they was slipping that rope under his neck.

MRS. PETERS (*crossing slowly to table and placing shawl and apron on table with other clothing*): No, it's strange. It must have been done awful crafty and still. They say it was such a—funny way to kill a man, rigging it all up like that.

MRS. HALE (*crossing to left of Mrs. Peters at table*): That's just what Mr. Hale said. There was a gun in the house. He says that's what he can't understand.

MRS. PETERS: Mr. Henderson said coming out that what was needed for the case was a motive: something to show anger, or—sudden feeling.

MRS. HALE (*who is standing by the table*): Well, I don't see any signs of anger around here. (*She puts her hand on the dish towel, which lies on the table, stands looking down at table, one-half of which is clean, the other half messy.*) It's wiped to here. (*Makes a move as if to finish work, then turns and looks at loaf of bread outside the breadbox. Drops towel. In that voice of coming back to familiar things.*) Wonder how they are finding things upstairs. (*Crossing below table to down right.*) I hope she had it a little more red-up up there. You know, it seems kind of *sneaking*. Locking her up in town and then coming out here and trying to get her own house to turn against her!

MRS. PETERS: But, Mrs. Hale, the law is the law.

MRS. HALE: I s'pose 'tis. (*Unbuttoning her coat.*) Better loosen up your things, Mrs. Peters. You won't feel them when you go out. (*Mrs. Peters takes off her fur tippet, goes to hang it on chair back left of table, stands looking at the work basket on floor near down left window.*)

MRS. PETERS: She was piecing a quilt. (*She brings the large sewing basket to the center table and they look at the bright pieces, Mrs. Hale above the table and Mrs. Peters left of it.*)

MRS. HALE: It's a log cabin pattern. Pretty, isn't it? I wonder if she was goin' to quilt it or just knot it? (*Footsteps have been heard coming down the stairs. The Sheriff enters followed by Hale and the County Attorney.*)

SHERIFF: They wonder if she was going to quilt it or just knot it! (*The men laugh, the women look abashed.*)

COUNTY ATTORNEY (*rubbing his hands over the stove*): Frank's fire didn't do much up there, did it? Well, let's go out to the barn and get that cleared up. (*The men go outside by up left door.*)

MRS. HALE (*resentfully*): I don't know as there's anything so strange, our takin' up our time with little things while we're waiting for them to get the evidence. (*She sits in chair right of table smoothing out a block with decision.*) I don't see as it's anything to laugh about.

MRS. PETERS (*apologetically*): Of course they've got awful important things on their minds. (*Pulls up a chair and joins Mrs. Hale at the left of the table.*)

MRS. HALE (*examining another block*): Mrs. Peters, look at this one. Here, this is the one she was working on, and look at the sewing! All the rest of it has been so nice and even. And look at this! It's all over the place! Why, it looks as if she didn't know what she was about! (*After she has said this they look at each other, then start to glance back at the door. After an instant Mrs. Hale has pulled at a knot and ripped the sewing.*)

MRS. PETERS: Oh, what are you doing, Mrs. Hale?

MRS. HALE (*mildly*): Just pulling out a stitch or two that's not sewed very good. (*Threading a needle.*) Bad sewing always made me fidgety.

MRS. PETERS (*with a glance at the door, nervously*): I don't think we ought to touch things.

MRS. HALE: I'll just finish up this end. (*Suddenly stopping and leaning forward.*) Mrs. Peters?

MRS. PETERS: Yes, Mrs. Hale?

MRS. HALE: What do you suppose she was so nervous about?

MRS. PETERS: Oh—I don't know. I don't know as she was nervous. I sometimes sew awful queer when I'm just tired. (*Mrs. Hale starts to say something, looks at Mrs. Peters, then goes on sewing.*) Well, I must get these things wrapped up. They may be through sooner than we think. (*Putting apron and other things together.*) I wonder where I can find a piece of paper, and string. (*Rises.*)

MRS. HALE: In that cupboard, maybe.

MRS. PETERS (*crosses right looking in cupboard*): Why, here's a bird-cage. (*Holds it up.*) Did she have a bird, Mrs. Hale?

MRS. HALE: Why, I don't know whether she did or not—I've not been here for so long. There was a man around last year selling canaries cheap, but I don't know as she took one; maybe she did. She used to sing real pretty herself.

MRS. PETERS (*glancing around*): Seems funny to think of a bird here. But she must have had one, or why would she have a cage? I wonder what happened to it?

MRS. HALE: I s'pose maybe the cat got it.

MRS. PETERS: No, she didn't have a cat. She's got that feeling some people have about cats—being afraid of them. My cat got in her room and she was real upset and asked me to take it out.

MRS. HALE: My sister Bessie was like that. Queer, ain't it?

MRS. PETERS (*examining the cage*): Why, look at this door. It's broke. One hinge is pulled apart. (*Takes a step down to Mrs. Hale's right.*)

MRS. HALE (*looking too*): Looks as if someone must have been rough with it.

MRS. PETERS: Why, yes. (*She brings the cage forward and puts it on the table.*)

MRS. HALE (*glancing toward up left door*): I wish if they're going to find any evidence they'd be about it. I don't like this place.

MRS. PETERS: But I'm awful glad you came with me, Mrs. Hale. It would be lonesome for me sitting here alone.

MRS. HALE: It would, wouldn't it? (*Dropping her sewing.*) But I tell you what I do wish, Mrs. Peters. I wish I had come over sometimes when *she* was here. I—(*looking around the room*)—wish I had.

MRS. PETERS: But of course you were awful busy, Mrs. Hale—your house and your children.

MRS. HALE (*rises and crosses left*): I could've come. I stayed away because it weren't cheerful—and that's why I ought to have come. I—(*looking out left window*)—I've never liked this place. Maybe it's because it's down in a hollow and you don't see the road. I dunno what it is, but it's a lonesome place and always was. I wish I had come over to see Minnie Foster sometimes. I can see now—(*Shakes her head.*)

MRS. PETERS (*left of table and above it*): Well, you mustn't reproach yourself, Mrs. Hale. Somehow we just don't see how it is with other folks until—something turns up.

MRS. HALE: Not having children makes less work—but it makes a quiet house, and Wright out to work all day, and no company when he did come in. (*Turning from window.*) Did you know John Wright, Mrs. Peters?

MRS. PETERS: Not to know him; I've seen him in town. They say he was a good man.

MRS. HALE: Yes—good; he didn't drink, and kept his word as well as most, I guess, and paid his debts. But he was a hard man, Mrs. Peters. Just to pass the time of day with him—(*Shivers.*) Like a raw wind that gets to the bone. (*Pauses, her eye falling on the cage.*) I should think she would 'a' wanted a bird. But what do you suppose went with it?

MRS. PETERS: I don't know, unless it got sick and died. (*She reaches over and swings the broken door, swings it again, both women watch it.*)

MRS. HALE: You weren't raised round here, were you? (*Mrs. Peters shakes her head.*) You didn't know—her?

MRS. PETERS: Not till they brought her yesterday.

MRS. HALE: She—come to think of it, she was kind of like a bird herself—real sweet and pretty, but kind of timid and—fluttery. How—she—did—change. (*Silence: then as if struck by a happy thought and relieved to get back to everyday things. Crosses right above Mrs. Peters to cupboard, replaces small chair used to stand on to its original place down right.*) Tell you what, Mrs. Peters, why don't you take the quilt in with you? It might take up her mind.

MRS. PETERS: Why, I think that's a real nice idea, Mrs. Hale. There couldn't possibly be any objection to it could there? Now, just what would I take? I wonder if her patches are in here—and her things. (*They look in the sewing basket.*)

MRS. HALE (*crosses to right of table*): Here's some red. I expect this has got sewing things in it. (*Brings out a fancy box.*) What a pretty box. Looks like something somebody would give you. Maybe her scissors are in here. (*Opens box. Suddenly puts her hand to her nose.*) Why——(*Mrs. Peters bends nearer, then turns her face away.*) There's something wrapped up in this piece of silk.

MRS. PETERS: Why, this isn't her scissors.

MRS. HALE (*lifting the silk*): Oh, Mrs. Peters—it's———(*Mrs. Peters bends closer.*)

MRS. PETERS: It's the bird.

MRS. HALE: But, Mrs. Peters—look at it! Its neck! Look at its neck! It's all—other side *to*.

MRS. PETERS: Somebody—wrung—its—neck. (*Their eyes meet. A look of growing comprehension, of horror. Steps are heard outside. Mrs. Hale slips box under quilt pieces, and sinks into her chair. Enter Sheriff and County Attorney. Mrs. Peters steps down left and stands looking out of window.*)

COUNTY ATTORNEY (*as one turning from serious things to little pleasantries*): Well, ladies, have you decided whether she was going to quilt it or knot it? (*Crosses to center above table.*)

MRS. PETERS: We think she was going to—knot it. (*Sheriff crosses to right of stove, lifts stove lid, and glances at fire, then stands warming hands at stove.*)

COUNTY ATTORNEY: Well, that's interesting, I'm sure. (*Seeing the bird-cage.*) Has the bird flown?

MRS. HALE (*putting more quilt pieces over the box*): We think the—cat got it.

COUNTY ATTORNEY (*preoccupied*): Is there a cat? (*Mrs. Hale glances in a quick covert way at Mrs. Peters.*)

MRS. PETERS (*turning from window takes a step in*): Well, not *now*. They're superstitious, you know. They leave.

COUNTY ATTORNEY (*to Sheriff Peters, continuing an interrupted conversation*): No sign at all of anyone having come from the outside. Their own rope. Now let's go up again and go over it piece by piece. (*They start upstairs.*) It would have to have been someone who knew just the———(*Mrs. Peters sits down left of table. The two women sit there not looking at one another, but as if peering into something and at the same time holding back. When they talk now it is in the manner of feeling their way over strange ground, as if afraid of what they are saying, but as if they cannot help saying it.*)

MRS. HALE (*hesitatively and in hushed voice*): She liked the bird. She was going to bury it in that pretty box.

MRS. PETERS (*in a whisper*): When I was a girl—my kitten—there was a boy took a hatchet, and before my eyes—and before I could get there———(*Covers her face an instant.*) If they hadn't held me back I would have—(*catches herself, looks upstairs where steps are heard, falters weakly*)—hurt him.

MRS. HALE (*with a slow look around her*): I wonder how it would seem never to have had any children around. (*Pause.*) No, Wright wouldn't like the bird—a thing that sang. She used to sing. He killed that, too.

MRS. PETERS (*moving uneasily*): We don't know who killed the bird.

MRS. HALE: I knew John Wright.

MRS. PETERS: It was an awful thing was done in this house that night, Mrs. Hale. Killing a man while he slept, slipping a rope around his neck that choked the life out of him.

MRS. HALE: His neck. Choked the life out of him. (*Her hand goes out and rests on the bird-cage.*)

MRS. PETERS (*with rising voice*): We don't know who killed him. We don't *know*.

MRS. HALE (*her own feelings not interrupted*): If there'd been years and years of nothing, then a bird to sing to you, it would be awful—still, after the bird was still.

MRS. PETERS (*something within her speaking*): I know what stillness is. When we homesteaded in Dakota, and my first baby died—after he was two years old, and me with no other then——

MRS. HALE (*moving*): How soon do you suppose they'll be through looking for the evidence?

MRS. PETERS: I know what stillness is. (*Pulling herself back.*) The law has got to punish crimes, Mrs. Hale.

MRS. HALE (*not as if answering that*): I wish you'd seen Minnie Foster when she wore a white dress with blue ribbons and stood up there in the choir and sang. (*A look around the room.*) Oh, I *wish* I'd come over here once in a while! That was a crime! That was a crime! Who's going to punish that?

MRS. PETERS (*looking upstairs*): We mustn't—take on.

MRS. HALE: I might have known she needed help! I know how things can be—for women. I tell you, it's queer, Mrs. Peters. We live close together and we live far apart. We all go through the same things— it's all just a different kind of the same thing. (*Brushes her eyes, noticing the jar of fruit, reaches out for it.*) If I was you I wouldn't tell her her fruit was gone. Tell her it *ain't*. Tell her it's all right. Take this in to prove it to her. She—she may never know whether it was broke or not.

MRS. PETERS (*takes the jar, looks about for something to wrap it in; takes petticoat from the clothes brought from the other room, very nervously begins winding this around the jar. In a false voice*): My, it's a good thing the men couldn't hear us. Wouldn't they just laugh! Getting all stirred up over a little thing like a—dead canary. As if that could have anything to do with—with—wouldn't they *laugh*! (*The men are heard coming downstairs.*)

MRS. HALE (*under her breath*): Maybe they would—maybe they wouldn't.

COUNTY ATTORNEY: No, Peters, it's all perfectly clear except a reason for doing it. But you know juries when it comes to women. If there was some definite thing. (*Crosses slowly to above table. Sheriff crosses down right. Mrs. Hale and Mrs. Peters remain seated at either side of table.*) Something to show—something to make a story about—a thing that would connect up with this strange way of doing it———(*The women's eyes meet for an instant. Enter Hale from outer door.*)

HALE (*remaining by door*): Well, I've got the team around. Pretty cold out there.

COUNTY ATTORNEY: I'm going to stay awhile by myself. (*To the Sheriff.*) You can send Frank out for me, can't you? I want to go over everything. I'm not satisfied that we can't do better.

SHERIFF: Do you want to see what Mrs. Peters is going to take in? (*The Lawyer picks up the apron, laughs.*)

COUNTY ATTORNEY: Oh, I guess they're not very dangerous things the ladies have picked out. (*Moves a few things about, disturbing the quilt pieces which cover the box. Steps back.*) No, Mrs. Peters doesn't need supervising. For that matter a sheriff's wife is married to the law. Ever think of it that way, Mrs. Peters?

MRS. PETERS: Not—just that way.

SHERIFF (*chuckling*): Married to the law. (*Moves to down right door to the other room.*) I just want you to come in here a minute, George. We ought to take a look at these windows.

COUNTY ATTORNEY (*scoffingly*): Oh, windows!

SHERIFF: We'll be right out, Mr. Hale. (*Hale goes outside. The Sheriff follows the County Attorney into the room. Then Mrs. Hale rises, hands tight together, looking intensely at Mrs. Peters, whose eyes make a slow turn, finally meeting Mrs. Hale's. A moment Mrs. Hale holds her, then her own eyes point the way to where the box is concealed. Suddenly Mrs. Peters throws back quilt pieces and tries to put the box in the bag she is carrying. It is too big. She opens box, starts to take bird out, cannot touch it, goes to pieces, stands there helpless. Sound of a knob turning in the other room. Mrs. Hale snatches the box and puts it in the pocket of her big coat. Enter County Attorney and Sheriff, who remains down right.*)

COUNTY ATTORNEY (*crosses to up left door facetiously*): Well, Henry, at least we found out that she was not going to quilt it. She was going to—what is it you call it, ladies?

MRS. HALE (*standing center below table facing front, her hand against her pocket*): We call it—knot it, Mr. Henderson.

[1916]

QUESTIONS ABOUT THE PLAY

- [ ] What do the stage directions reveal about the **setting** and the **characters**? How affluent are these characters? What do they wear, and how do they carry themselves? Do you get a sense of where this play might take place? What is the effect of these details?

- [ ] What kind of **diction** do characters use in *Trifles*? Elevated? Conversational? A mixture of both?

- [ ] *Trifles* does not, at first, seem like a play full of sensational **spectacles**. But what elements in this play surprise you as you read about them? How does it affect the **characters'** exploration of the play's **themes**?

SAMPLE PAPER: AN ANALYSIS

Sarah Johnson was free to choose the topic and focus of her paper. In the same semester as her literature class, she was enrolled in a philosophy course on ethics where she was introduced to the idea of situational ethics, the notion that exterior pressures often cause people to act in ways they might normally deem unethical, often to prevent or allay a worse evil. This philosophical concept was on Sarah's mind when she read *Trifles*. She noticed that the character of Mrs. Peters does indeed end up behaving in a way she would probably never have imagined for herself. This seemed an interesting concept to pursue, so Sarah decided to trace the development of Mrs. Peters's journey away from her original moral certainty.

Sarah Johnson

English 253

Professor Riley

24 October 2007

Moral Ambiguity and Character Development

in *Trifles*

What is the relationship between legality and morality?
Susan Glaspell's short play *Trifles* asks us to ponder this question,
but it provides no clear answers. Part murder mystery, part battle
of the sexes, the play makes its readers confront and question
many issues about laws, morals, and human relationships. In the
person of Mrs. Peters, a sheriff's wife, the play chronicles one
woman's moral journey from a certain, unambiguous belief in the
law to a more situational view of ethics. Before it is over, this
once legally minded woman is even willing to cover up the truth
and let someone get away with murder.

*Sarah focuses on
Mrs. Peters right
away.*

At the beginning of the play, Mrs. Peters believes that law,
truth, and morality are one and the same. Though never unkind
about the accused, Mrs. Wright, Mrs. Peters is at first firm in her
belief that the men will find the truth and crime will be punished
as it should be. Mrs. Hale feels the men are "kind of *sneaking*" as
they look about Mrs. Wright's abandoned house for evidence
against her, but Mrs. Peters assures her that "the law is the law."
It is not that Mrs. Peters is less sympathetic toward women than
her companion, but she is even more sympathetic toward the
lawmen, because her version of morality is so absolute. When the
men deride the women's interest in so-called trifles, like sewing
and housework, Mrs. Hale takes offense. But Mrs. Peters, convinced that the law must prevail, defends them, saying, "It's no
more than their duty," and later, "They've got awful important
things on their minds."

*Sarah uses direct
quotations from
the play text as
backup for her
claims.*

As she attempts to comply with the requirements of the law,
Mrs. Peters is described in a stage direction as "businesslike,"

and she tries to maintain a skeptical attitude as she waits for the truth to emerge. Asked if she thinks Mrs. Wright killed her husband, she says "Oh, I don't know." She seems to be trying to convince herself that the accused is innocent until proven guilty, though she admits that her husband thinks it "looks bad for her." She seems to have absorbed her husband's attitudes and values and to be keeping a sort of legalistic distance from her feelings about the case.

Mrs. Hale is less convinced of the rightness of the men or the law. Even before the two women discover a possible motive for the murder, Mrs. Hale is already tampering with evidence, tearing out the erratic sewing stitches that suggest Mrs. Wright was agitated. Mrs. Peters says, "I don't think we ought to touch things," but she doesn't make any stronger move to stop Mrs. Hale, who continues to fix the sewing. At this point, we see her first beginning to waver from her previously firm stance on right and wrong.

It is not that Mrs. Peters is unsympathetic to the hard life that Mrs. Wright has led. She worries with Mrs. Hale about the accused woman's frozen jars of preserves, her half-done bread, and her unfinished quilt. But she tries to think, like the men, that these things are "trifles" and that what matters is the legal truth. But when she sees a bird with a wrung neck, things begin to change in a major way. She remembers the boy who killed her kitten when she was a child, and the sympathy she has felt for Mrs. Wright begins to turn to empathy. The empathy is enough to cause her first lie to the men. When the county attorney spies the empty bird cage, she corroborates Mrs. Hale's story about a cat getting the bird, even though she knows there was no cat in the house.

Even after she has reached that point of empathy, Mrs. Peters tries hard to maintain her old way of thinking and of being. Alone again with Mrs. Hale, she says firmly, "We don't know who killed the bird," even though convincing evidence

In this para-
graph, Sar
analyzes a
ing point i
play text:
moment c
Mrs. Peter
experienc
transform

points to John Wright. More important, she says of Wright himself, "We don't know who killed him. We don't *know*." But her repetition and her "rising voice," described in a stage direction, show how agitated she has become. As a believer in the law, she should feel certain that everyone is innocent until proven guilty, but she thinks she knows the truth, and, perhaps for the first time in her life, legal truth does not square with moral truth. Her empathy deepens further still when she thinks about the stillness of the house in which Mrs. Wright was forced to live after the death of her beloved pet, who brought song to an otherwise grim life. She knows Mrs. Wright is childless, and she now remembers not just the death of her childhood kitten but also the terrible quiet in her own house after her first child died. She reaches a moment of crisis between her two ways of thinking when she says, "I know what stillness is. (*Pulling herself back.*) The law has got to punish crimes, Mrs. Hale." This is perhaps the most important line in the chronicle of her growth as a character. First she expresses her newfound empathy with the woman she believes to be a murderer; then, as the stage directions say, she tries to pull herself back and return to the comfortable moral certainty that she felt just a short time before. It is too late for that, though.

Here and elsewhere, Sarah relies on stage directions as evidence for her claims about Mrs. Peters.

Sarah isolates this passage to emphasize the complexity of Mrs. Peters.

In the end, Mrs. Peters gives in to what she believes to be emotionally right rather than what is legally permissible. She collaborates with Mrs. Hale to cover up evidence of the motive and hide the dead canary. Though very little time has gone by, she has undergone a major transformation. She may be, as the county attorney says, "married to the law," but she is also divorced from her old ideals. When she tries to cover up the evidence, a stage direction says she "goes to pieces," and Mrs. Hale has to help her. By the time she pulls herself together, the new woman she is will be a very different person from the old one. She, along with the reader, is now in a world where the relationship between legality and morality is far more complex than she had ever suspected.

CHAPTER 7

Writing a Literary Research Paper

Writing a literary research paper draws on the same set of skills as writing any other paper—choosing a topic, developing a thesis, gathering and organizing support, and so on. The main difference between research writing and other sorts of writing lies in the number and types of sources from which one's support comes. All writing about literature begins with a **primary source**—the poem, story, or play on which the writing is based. Research papers also incorporate **secondary sources**, such as biographical, historical, and critical essays.

The most important thing to remember as you begin the process of research writing is that you are writing a critical argument. Your paper should not end up reading like a book report or a catalog of what others have said about the literature. Rather, it should begin and end by making an original point based on your own ideas, and like any other paper, it needs a clear, sharply focused thesis. The sources, both primary and secondary, are there to support your thesis, not to take over the paper.

The method laid out below seems very linear and straightforward: find and evaluate sources for your paper, read them and take notes, and then write a paper integrating material from these sources. In reality, the process is rarely, if ever, this neat. As you read and write, you will discover gaps in your knowledge or you will ask yourself new questions that will demand more research. Be flexible. Keep in mind that the process of research is recursive, requiring a writer to move back and forth between various stages. Naturally, this means that for research writing, even more than for other kinds of writing, you should start early and give yourself plenty of time to complete the project.

FINDING SOURCES

For many students, research is more or less synonymous with the Internet. There is a widely held perception that all the information anybody could ever want is available online, readily and easily accessible. But

110

when it comes to literary research, this is not the case at all. True, there are plenty of Web sites and newsgroups devoted to literary figures, but the type of information available on these sites tends to be limited to a narrow range—basic biographies of authors, plot summaries, and so forth—and the quality of information is highly variable. Though serious literary scholarship does exist online, print books and journals are still the better sources for you in most cases.

Books

The place to begin your search, then, is with your college or university library's catalog. (Public libraries, no matter how well-run, seldom carry the scholarly journals and other sorts of specialized sources needed for college-level research.) Start by looking for one or two good books on your topic. Books tend to be more general in their scope than journal articles, and they can be especially useful at the early stages of your research to help you focus and refine your thinking. If you have given yourself sufficient time for the process, take a book or two home and skim them to determine which parts would be most useful for you. When you return to the library to perform more research, you will have a clearer sense of what you are looking for and will be therefore more efficient at completing the rest of your search.

Periodicals

Next, look at periodicals. At this point, you should be aware of the distinction between **magazines**, which are directed at a general readership, and **scholarly journals**, which are written by and for specialists in various academic fields. *Scientific American*, for instance, is a well-respected magazine available on newsstands, whereas *The Journal of Physical Chemistry* is a scholarly journal, generally available only by subscription and read more or less exclusively by chemists and chemistry students. In the field of literary studies there are literally hundreds of journals, ranging from publications covering a general period or topic (*American Literary Realism, Modern Drama*) to those devoted to specific authors (*Walt Whitman Review, Melville Society Extracts*).

While magazines like *Time* and *Newsweek* are sometimes appropriate research sources, and you certainly should not rule them out, the highest quality and most sophisticated literary criticism tends to appear in journals. If you are uncertain whether you are looking at a scholarly journal, look for the following typical characteristics:

- Scholarly journal articles tend to be *longer* than magazine articles, ranging anywhere from five to more than fifty pages.

- Journal articles are *written by specialists* for researchers, professors, and college students. The author's professional credentials and institutional affiliation are often listed.

- Journal articles tend to be written in a given profession's *special language* and can be difficult for nonspecialists to understand. Articles in literary journals use the specialized language of literary theory and criticism.

- Journal articles are usually *peer-reviewed* or refereed, meaning that other specialists have read them and determined that they make a significant contribution to the field. Peer referees are often listed as an editorial board on the journal's masthead page.

- Journal articles usually include *footnotes or endnotes* and an often substantial references, *bibliography*, or works cited section.

Online Indexes

Your college library is likely to subscribe to a number of services that index journal and magazine articles in order to help researchers find what they are looking for. Some of the most useful indexes for literary research are the *MLA International Bibliography*, the *Humanities Index* (published by H. W. Wilson), and the *Expanded Academic ASAP* (from InfoTRAC). If you do not know how to access these sources, ask the reference librarian on duty at your college library. Helping students find what they need is this person's principal job, and you will likely learn a lot from him or her. Both your librarian and your instructor can also suggest additional indexes to point you toward good secondary sources.

When you begin searching, be prepared with fairly specific search terms to help the database focus on what you really need and to filter out irrelevant material. Let's say you are researching the nature of love in Shakespeare's sonnets. If you perform a search on the keyword or topic *Shakespeare*, you will get thousands of hits, many of them about topics unrelated to yours. Searching on both *Shakespeare* and *sonnet*, however, will get you closer to what you want, while searching on *Shakespeare*, *sonnet*, and *love* will yield far fewer and far better, targeted results. If your search nets you fewer results than you expected, try again with different terms (substitute *romance* for *love*, for example). Be patient, and don't be afraid to ask your instructor or librarian for help if you are experiencing difficulty.

Once you have a screen full of results, you will be able to access a **text**, an **abstract**, or a **citation**. Some results will give you a link to the complete text of an article; just click on the link and you can read the article on-screen, print it out, or e-mail it to yourself. Frequently, a link is provided to an abstract of the article, a brief summary (generally just a few sentences) that overviews the content of the full article. Reading an abstract is a very good way of finding out whether it is worth tracking down the whole article for your paper. A citation gives only the most basic information about an article—its title, author, the date of publication, and its page numbers—and it is up to you to then find and read the whole article.

It may be tempting to settle on only those articles available immediately in full-text versions. Don't fall into this trap. As we mentioned earlier, many of the best sources of literary research are available only in print, and the only way to get to these is to follow the citation's lead and locate the journal in the library stacks. If a title or abstract looks promising, go and retrieve the article. If you think getting up and tracking down a journal is frustrating or time-consuming, imagine how frustrating and time-consuming it will be to attempt writing a research paper without great sources.

Interlibrary Loan

If you find a promising lead but discover your library doesn't have a particular book or has no subscription to the needed periodical, you still may be in luck. Nearly all libraries offer **interlibrary loan** services, which can track down books and articles from a large network of other libraries and send them to your home institution, generally free of charge. Of course, this process takes time—usually, a couple of days to a couple of weeks—and this is yet another reason to get started as early as possible on your research.

The Internet

Lastly, if your quest for books and periodicals has not yielded all the results you want, search the World Wide Web. As with a search of a specialized index, you will do better and filter out a lot of the low-quality sources if you come up with some well-focused search terms in advance. Be sure to ask your instructor or reference librarian about authoritative Web sites. Your librarian may have already created a special page on the library's Web site that provides links to the best Web sites for students of English. If you use the Web for your research, look especially for scholarly sites, written by professors or researchers and maintained by colleges and universities. For example, if you want to research the poetry and artwork of William Blake, you might check The Blake Archive, an online project sponsored by the Library of Congress and UNC Chapel Hill: http://www.blakearchive.org/blake/. If you are interested in learning

more about Walt Whitman's life and work, check The Walt Whitman Archive, a project developed and edited by Ed Folsom and Kenneth M. Price, both of whom are eminent Whitman scholars: http://www .whitmanarchive.org/. If you want to read the 1603 printing of *Hamlet*, check the British Library's Web site: http://www.bl.uk/treasures/ shakespeare/homepage.html. Also potentially useful are the online equivalents of scholarly journals, as well as discussion groups or newsgroups dedicated to particular authors, literary schools, or periods.

EVALUATING SOURCES

As you locate **research sources**, you should engage in a continual process of evaluation to determine both the reliability of the potential source and its appropriateness to your particular topic and needs. Keep the following questions in mind to help you evaluate both print and electronic sources.

- **Who is the author, and what are his or her credentials?** If this information is not readily available, you might ask yourself why not. Is the author or publisher trying to hide something?
- **What is the medium of publication?** Books, journals, magazines, newspapers, and electronic publications all have something to offer a researcher, but they do not all offer the same thing. A good researcher will usually seek out a variety of sources.
- **How respectable is the publisher?** Not all publishers are created equal, and some have a much better reputation than others for reliability. Just because something is published, that doesn't make it accurate—think of all those supermarket tabloids publishing articles about alien autopsies. In general, your best sources are books from university presses and major, well-established publishers; scholarly journal articles; and articles from well-regarded magazines and newspapers such as the *Atlantic Monthly* or the *New York Times*. If you are not sure how respectable or reliable a particular publisher or source might be, ask your instructor or librarian.
- **If it's an online publication, who is hosting the site?** Though commercial sites (whose Web addresses end in *.com*) should not be ruled out, keep in mind that these sites are often driven by profit as much as a desire to educate the public. Sites hosted by educational institutions, nonprofit organizations, or the government (*.edu*, *.org*, and *.gov*, respectively) tend to be more purely educational.
- **How recent is the publication?** While there are many instances in which older publications are appropriate—you may be doing

historical research or you may want to refer to a classic in a certain field—newer ones are preferable, all other things being equal. Newer publications take advantage of more recent ideas and theories, and they often summarize or incorporate older sources.

- **How appropriate is the source to your specific project?** Even the highest quality scholarly journal or a book by the top expert in a given field will be appropriate only for a very limited number of research projects. Let your topic, your tentative thesis, and your common sense be your guides.

How do you know when you have enough sources? Many instructors specify a minimum number of sources for research papers, and many students find exactly that number of sources and then look no further. Your best bet is to stop looking for sources when you really believe you have enough material to write a top-quality paper. Indeed, it is far better to gather up too many sources and end up not using them all than to get too few and find yourself wanting more information as you write. And remember that any "extra" research beyond what you actually cite in your paper isn't really wasted effort—every piece of information you read contributes to your background knowledge and overall understanding of your topic, making your final paper sound smarter and better informed.

WORKING WITH SOURCES

You now have a stack of books, articles, and printouts of electronic sources. How do you work through these to get the support you need for your paper?

- *First*, sort the various sources by expected relevance, with those you think will be most informative and useful to you on the top of the list.
- *Then*, skim or read through everything quickly, highlighting or making note of the parts that seem most directly applicable to your paper. (Obviously, you should not mark up or otherwise deface library materials—take notes on a separate page.)
- *Then* slow down and reread the important passages again, this time taking careful notes.
- *Keep* yourself scrupulously well organized at this point, making sure that you always know which of your notes refers to which source.

If you are taking notes by hand, it's a good idea to start a separate page for each source. If you are using a computer to take notes, start a separate file or section for each new source you read.

Notes will generally fall into one of four categories: quotations, paraphrases, summaries, and commentaries.

Quoting

[margin note: Use only a few small quotes]

While **quotations** are useful, and you will almost certainly incorporate several into your paper, resist the urge to transcribe large portions of text from your sources. Papers that rely too heavily on quotations can be unpleasant reading, with a cluttered or choppy style that comes from moving back and forth between your prose and that of the various authors you quote. Reserve direct quoting for those passages that are especially relevant and that you simply can't imagine phrasing as clearly or elegantly yourself. When you do make note of a quotation, be sure also to note the pages on which it appears in the source material so that later you will be able to cite it accurately.

Paraphrasing and Summarizing

[margin note: Use these more often than quotes.]

Most often, you should take notes in the form of **paraphrase** or summary. To paraphrase, simply put an idea or opinion drawn from a source into your own words. Generally, a paraphrase will be about equal in length to the passage being paraphrased, while a summary will be much shorter, capturing the overall point of a passage while leaving out supporting details. Paraphrasing and summarizing are usually superior to quoting for two reasons. First, if you can summarize or paraphrase with confidence, then you know you have really understood what you have read. Second, a summary or paraphrase will be more easily transferred from your notes to your paper and will fit in well with your individual prose style. Just as with quotations, make a note of the page numbers in the source material from which your summaries and paraphrases are drawn.

Commenting

[margin note: they'll keep you from just copying the others]

Finally, some of your notes can be written as **commentaries**. When something you read strikes you as interesting, you can record your reaction to it. Do you agree or disagree strongly? Why? What exactly is the connection between the source material and your topic or tentative thesis? Making copious commentaries will help you to keep your own ideas in the forefront and will keep your paper from devolving into a shopping list of other writers' priorities. Be sure to note carefully when you are commenting rather than summarizing or paraphrasing. When you are drafting your paper, you will want to distinguish carefully between which ideas are your own and which are borrowed from others.

outline: phrases

beware of "about" in thesis.   WRITING THE PAPER   117

Keeping Track of Your Sources

As you take notes on the substance of your reading, it is also essential *make sure you can easily get the source* that you record the source's author, title, and publication information for later use in compiling your works cited list, or bibliography. Nothing is more frustrating than having to return to the library or retrace your research steps on a computer just to get a page reference or the full title of a source. Most accomplished researchers actually put together their works cited list as they go along rather than waiting until the essay is drafted. Such a strategy will ensure you have all the information you need, and it will save you from the painstaking (and potentially tedious) task of having to create the list all at once at the end of your process.

WRITING THE PAPER

After what may seem like a long time spent gathering and working with your sources, you are now ready to begin the actual writing of your paper.

Refine Your Thesis

Start by looking again at your tentative thesis. Now that you have read a lot and know much more about your topic, does your proposed thesis still seem compelling and appropriate? Is it a little too obvious, something that other writers have already said or have taken for granted? Do you perhaps need to refine or modify it in order to take into account the information you have learned and opinions you have encountered? If necessary—and it usually is—refine or revise your tentative thesis so it can help you stay focused as you write. *make sure it's what you want to write about*

Organize Your Evidence

Next you will need, just as with any other essay, to organize the supporting evidence of your thesis. Follow whatever process for organization you have used successfully in writing other papers, while bearing in mind that this time you will likely have more, and more complex, evidence to deal with. You likely will need an outline—formal or informal—to help you put your materials in a coherent and sensible order. But, once again, flexibility is the key here. If, as you begin to work your way through the outline, some different organizational strategy begins to make sense to you, revise your outline rather than forcing your ideas into a preconceived format. *treat it like another essay*

Start Your Draft

The actual drafting of the research paper is probably the part you will find most similar to writing other papers. Try to write fairly quickly and fluently, knowing you can and will add examples, fill in explanations, eliminate redundancies, and work on style during the revision phase. As with your other papers, you may want to write straight through from beginning to end, or you may want to save difficult passages like the introduction for last. Interestingly, many writers find that the process of drafting a research paper actually goes a bit more quickly than does drafting other papers, largely because their considerable research work has left them so well-versed in the topic that they have a wealth of ideas for writing.

What might slow you down as you draft your research papers are the citations, which you provide so that a reader knows which ideas are your own and which come from outside sources. Before you begin drafting, familiarize yourself with the conventions for MLA in-text citations. Each time you incorporate a quotation, paraphrase, or summary into your essay, you will need to cite the author's name and the relevant page numbers from the source material. Do not, however, get hung up at this stage trying to remember how to punctuate citations and so forth. There will be time to hammer out these details later, and it is important as you write to keep your focus on the big picture.

Revise

As you go through the revision process, you should do so with an eye toward full integration of your source material. Are all connections between quotations, paraphrases, or summaries and your thesis clear? Do you include sufficient commentary explaining the inclusion of all source material? Is it absolutely clear which ideas come from which research source? Most important, is the paper still a well-focused argument, meant to convince an audience of the validity of your original thesis? Bearing these questions in mind, you will be ready to make the same sorts of global revision decisions that you would for any other paper—what to add, what to cut, how to reorganize, and so forth.

Edit and Proofread

During the final editing and proofreading stage, include one editorial pass just for checking quotations and documentation format. Make sure each quotation is accurate and exact. Ensure that each reference to a source has an appropriate in-text citation and that your list of work cited (bibliography) is complete and correct. Double-check manuscrip

format and punctuation issues with the guidelines included in this book
or with another appropriate resource. After putting so much time and
effort into researching and writing your paper, it would be a shame to
have its effectiveness diminished by small inaccuracies or errors.

[handwritten margin note: you / That.]

UNDERSTANDING AND AVOIDING PLAGIARISM

Everyone knows that **plagiarism** is wrong. Buying or borrowing someone else's work, downloading all or part of a paper from the Web, and
similar practices are beyond reprehensible. Most colleges and universities have codes of academic honesty forbidding such practices and
imposing severe penalties—including expulsion from the institution in
some cases—on students who are caught breaking them. Many educa-
tors feel these penalties are, if anything, not severe enough. Instructors
tend to be not only angered but also baffled by students who plagiarize.
In addition to the obvious wrongs of cheating and lying (nobody likes
being lied to), students who plagiarize are losing out on a learning
opportunity, a waste of the student's time as well as the instructor's.

[handwritten margin note: moral of the story: Don't do it.]

Not everyone, though, is altogether clear on what plagiarism entails,
and a good deal of plagiarism can actually be unintentional on the part
of the student. A working definition of plagiarism will help to clarify
what plagiarism is:

- presenting someone else's ideas as your own;
- using information from any print or electronic source without fully
  citing the source;
- buying or "borrowing" a paper from any source;
- submitting work that someone else has written, in whole or in part;
- having your work edited to the point that it is no longer your work;
- submitting the same paper for more than one class without the
  express permission of the instructors involved.

[handwritten margin note: there's a lot of these things.]

Some of this is obvious. You know it is cheating to have a friend do
your homework or to download a paper from the Web and submit it as
your own. But the first and last items on the list are not as clear-cut or
self-explanatory. What exactly does it mean to present someone else's
ideas as your own? Many students mistakenly believe that as long as
they rephrase an idea into their own words, they have done their part to
avoid plagiarism. This, however, is not true. Readers assume, and rea-
sonably so, that everything in your paper is a product of your own thinking, not just your own phrasing, unless you share credit with another by
documenting your source. No matter how it is phrased, an original idea

[handwritten margin note: yeah I do that some times.]

belongs to the person who first thought of it and wrote it down; in fact the notion of possession in this context is so strong that the term applied to such ownership is *intellectual property.*

it all counts as plagiarism which sucks.

As an analogy, imagine you invented a revolutionary product, patented it, and put it up for sale. The next week, you find that your neighbor has produced the same product, painted it a different color, changed the name, and is doing a booming business selling the product. Is your neighbor any less guilty of stealing your idea just because he or she is using a new name and color for the product? Of course not. Your intellectual property, the idea behind the product, has been stolen. And you are no less guilty of plagiarism if you glean a piece of information, an opinion, or even an abstract concept from another person, put it into your own words, and "sell" it in your paper without giving proper credit.

Let us say, for example, that you find this passage about William Butler Yeats:

> Religious by temperament but unable to accept orthodox Christianity, Yeats throughout his life explored esoteric philosophies in search of a tradition that would substitute for a lost religion. He became a member of the Theosophical Society and the Order of the Golden Dawn, two groups interested in Eastern occultism, and later developed a private system of symbols and mystical ideas.

Drawing from this passage, you write:

It's still (cheating?)

> Yeats rejected the Christianity of his native Ireland, but he became interested in occultism and Eastern philosophy. From these sources, he developed his own system of mystical symbols which he used in his poetry.

now do you not do this?

Clearly the words of this new passage are your own, and some elements of the original have been streamlined while other information has been added. However, the essential line of reasoning and the central point of both passages is largely the same. If this second passage appears in your paper without an acknowledgment of the original source, *this is plagiarism.*

Finally, let's look at the last item on the list: submitting the same paper for more than one class without the express permission of the instructors involved. Sometimes, you will find substantial overlap in the subject matter of two or more of your classes. A literature class, for instance, has elements of history, psychology, sociology, and other disciplines, and once in a while you might find yourself working on writing projects in courses that share common features. You might be tempted to let your research and writing in such a case do double duty, and there is not necessarily anything wrong with that. However, if you wish to write a paper on a single topic for more than one class, clear these plans with both instructors first. And, of course, even if you use the same research sources for both assignments, you will almost certainly need to write two separate essays, tailoring each to meet the specifications of individual classes and disciplines.

don't just assume you can

WHAT TO DOCUMENT AND WHAT *NOT* TO DOCUMENT

Everything borrowed from another source needs to be documented. Obviously, you should document every direct quotation of any length from primary or secondary sources. Equally important is the documentation of all your paraphrases and summaries of ideas, information, and opinions, citing authors and page numbers. The rule of thumb is that if you didn't make it up yourself, you should probably document it.

way to do it

The word *probably* in the previous sentence suggests that there are exceptions, and indeed there are. You do not need to document proverbial sayings ("Live and let live") or very familiar quotations ("I have a dream"), though in the case of the latter you may want to allude to the speaker in your text. You also do not need to document any information that can be considered **common knowledge**. Common knowledge here refers not only to information that you would expect nearly every adult to know immediately (that Shakespeare wrote *Hamlet*, for instance, or that George Washington was the first president of the United States). Common knowledge also encompasses undisputed information that you could look up in a general or specialized reference work. The average person on the street probably couldn't tell you that T. S. Eliot was born in 1888, but you don't need to say where that piece of information comes from, as it is widely available to anyone who wishes to find it.

only the "big" things.

Use both your common sense and your sense of fairness to make any necessary decisions about whether or not to document something. When in doubt, ask your instructor, and remember, it's better to document something unnecessarily than to be guilty of plagiarism.

true.

DOCUMENTING SOURCES: MLA FORMAT

This section includes information on how to document the following:

Some students seem to believe that English teachers find footnotes and bibliographies and textual citations fun and interesting. In truth, few people know better than those who have to teach it how tedious format and documentation can be for a writer. Chances are your instructor will insist that you document your sources. There are at least three reasons for this. First, a sense of fair play requires that we give proper credit to those whose ideas benefit us. Second, by documenting your sources, you make it possible for your readers to find the sources themselves and follow up if they become interested in something in your paper. Third, documenting your sources, and doing it accurately, enhances your credibility as a writer by highlighting your professionalism and thoroughness.

As you read the following pages, and as you work on **documenting sources** in your own papers, don't say that you don't get it or that you can't learn this. If you learned the difficult and abstract skills of reading and writing, you can certainly learn something as concrete as documentation. Actually, documentation is the easy part of research writing, since there is only one right way to do it. The hard part is the creative work of discovering and presenting your original ideas and integrating them fluently with the work of others. And, of course, there is no need to actually memorize the specifics of format. Nobody does. When you need to know how to cite an anonymous newspaper article or what to include in a bibliographic entry for a radio broadcast, for instance, you can look it up. That's what professional writers do all the time.

There are many different forms and formulas for documenting sources—the APA (American Psychological Association) format commonly used in the social sciences, the CBE (Council of Biology Editors) format used in the life sciences, the *Chicago (Chicago Manual of Style)* format used in history, and so on. Each system highlights the type of information most relevant to experts in a particular field. If you have received contradictory instructions about documentation format for research projects in the past—include dates in your in-text references or don't, use footnotes or use endnotes—chances are you were working in different documentation systems. The format most often used in the humanities is MLA, the system developed by the Modern Language Association.

MLA format breaks down into two main elements: in-text citations and a works cited list (bibliography). In-text citations are parenthetical references that follow each quotation, paraphrase, or summary and give the briefest possible information about the source, usually the author's last name and a page number. The works cited list, which comes at the end of the paper, gives more detailed information about all sources used. The idea is that a reader coming across a parenthetical reference in your text can easily turn to the works cited list and get full details about the type of publication from which the material comes, the date of publication, etc.

(Some writers make use of a third element of MLA style, content end-notes, which come between the end of the paper and the works cited list and contain extra information not readily integrated into the paper. Although you may use endnotes if you wish, they are not necessary.)

The following pages describe the major types of sources you are likely to encounter and how to reference those sources both in the text of your research paper and in your works cited list. The information here, how-ever, is not exhaustive. If you want to cite a source not covered here, or if you would like more information about MLA style and citation format, turn to:

> *MLA Handbook for Writers of Research Papers.* 7th ed. New York: MLA, 2009. Print.

In-Text Citations

The purpose of an in-text citation is to give a very brief acknowledgment of a source within the body of your essay. In MLA format, in-text cita-tions take the form of brief parenthetical interruptions directly following each quotation, paraphrase, or summary. Some students find these interruptions a bit distracting at first, but you will quickly find that you grow accustomed to them and that soon they will not slow your reading or comprehension. The explanations and examples of in-text citations that follow should cover most instances you will encounter.

Citing Author and Page Number in Parentheses

Typically, a citation will contain the last name of the author being cited and a page number. The first example here shows a direct quotation, the second a paraphrase.

> One reviewer referred to *Top Girls* as, "among other things, a critique of bourgeois feminism" (Munk 33).

> When English wool was in demand, the fens were rich, but for many years now they have been among the poorest regions in England (Chamberlain 13).

Coming across these references in your text, your readers will know that they can turn to your works cited list and find out the full names of Munk and Chamberlain, the titles of what they have written, and where and when the works were published.

Please note:

- **In-text references contain no extraneous words or punctuation.** There is no comma between the name and the page number. The word *page* or the abbreviation *p.* do not precede the number. There are no extra spaces, just the name and the number.
- **Quotation marks close *before* the citation.** The in-text citation is not part of a direct quotation, so it does not belong inside the quotation marks.
- **The period that ends the sentence is placed *after* the citation.** Probably the most common error students make in MLA in-text citation is to put the period (or other closing quotation mark) at the end of the quotation or paraphrase and then give the reference in parentheses. Doing so, however, makes the citation the beginning of the next sentence rather than the end of the one being cited.

Citing the Author in Body Text and Only the Page Number in Parentheses

If you have already named the author in your own text, for instance in a lead-in phrase, you do not need to repeat the name in parentheses, as your reader will already know which author to look for in your works cited. In this case, the parenthetical reference need only contain the page numbers. The two examples already given could be rewritten as follows:

Reviewer Erika Munk referred to *Top Girls* as, "among other things, a critique of bourgeois feminism" (33).

Martha Chamberlain writes that when English wool was in demand, the fens were rich, but for many years now they have been among the poorest regions in England (13).

Citing Multiple Pages in a Source

You may find yourself wanting to make a brief summary of an extended passage, in which case you might need to cite the inclusive pages of the summarized material.

John McGrath's Scottish theater company was destroyed by the end of government subsidies, as Elizabeth MacLennan chronicles in *The Moon Belongs to Everyone* (137-99).

Citing Multiple Sources at Once

Sometimes several different sources say roughly the same thing, or at least there is substantial overlap in the parts you want to cite. Following are two ways of handling this situation; use whichever one best suits your needs.

> This particular passage in the play has been the source of much critical speculation, especially by Freudian critics (Anders 19; Olsen 116; Smith 83-84; Watson 412).

> A number of Freudian critics have commented on this passage, including Anders (19), Olsen (116), Smith (83-84), and Watson (412).

Citing Two or More Sources by the Same Author

It is common for one author to write multiple books or articles on the same general topic, and you might want to use more than one of them in your paper. In this case, a shortened version of the title must appear in the parenthetical reference, to show which work by the author is being quoted or cited. In citations for an article and a book about playwright Caryl Churchill, both by the author Geraldine Cousin, one would give the first word of the work's title (other than *the* or *a*, etc.). As seen here, *Common* and *Churchill* are the first words in the title of the article and the book, respectively.

> Churchill claims that this sentiment was really expressed to her by one of the gangmasters she encountered in the fens (Cousin, "Common" 6).

> Churchill's notebooks from her visit to the fens record her seeing baby prams parked around the fields in which the women worked (Cousin, *Churchill* 47).

Note the comma between the author's name and the title. Note that these shortened titles are punctuated (with underscoring or quotation marks) just as they would be in the works cited list or elsewhere in your writing, in quotation marks for an article and in italics or underscored for a book.

If the author is named in a signal phrase, only the shortened title and page number are needed in the parenthetical reference.

> "Violence," says Ruby Cohn, "is the only recourse in these brutalized lives on the Fen" (*Retreats* 139).

Citing a Quotation or Source within a Source

On page 58 of his book about Margaret Thatcher, Charles Moser writes:

> In a speech to Parliament in June of 1983, Thatcher said, "A return
> to Victorian values will encourage personal responsibility, personal
> initiative, self-respect, and respect for others and their property."

Let us say you do not have the text of Thatcher's original speech and that Moser doesn't make reference to a primary source that you can track down. But Moser is a reliable author, so you believe the Thatcher quotation is accurate and want to use a portion of it in your paper. This is done by giving the original speaker's name (in this case Margaret Thatcher) in your text and using the abbreviation *qtd. in* and the author from whom you got the quote (in this case Charles Moser) in the parenthetical citation.

> These "Victorian values," Thatcher claimed, would "encourage personal
> responsibility, personal initiative, self-respect, and respect for others"
> (qtd. in Moser 58).

Preparing Your Works Cited List

It is a good idea to begin preparing your list of **works cited** during the research process, adding new entries each time you find a source that might be useful to you. That way, when the time comes to finalize your paper, you can just edit the list you already have, making sure it contains all the necessary entries and no extraneous ones, and checking each for accuracy and format. If you wait until the end to create your works cited list, you will have to compile the whole list from scratch at a time when you are most tired and therefore least able to focus your attention on this necessary, detailed work.

General Guidelines

- **Begin your list of works cited on a new page.** Continue paginating as you have throughout the paper, with your last name and the page number appearing in the upper right corner.
- **Center the heading Works Cited at the top of the page** in capitals and lowercase letters; do not use italics, boldface print, or quotation marks.
- **Arrange sources alphabetically, by the last name of the source's author** (or by title, in the case of anonymous works), regardless of the order in which they are cited in your paper.

- **Begin each entry flush with the left margin.** When an entry takes up more than one line, all lines after the first are indented one-half inch. (For an example, see the works cited list in the research paper by Jarrad Nunes, on p. 142.) This is called a hanging indent, and all major word processing programs can be set to format your entries this way.
- **Double-space the entire list.**
- **Do not put extra line spaces between entries.**
- **As always, carefully follow any additional or contrary instructions provided by your instructor.**

Citing Books

To list books in your works cited, include as much of the following information as is available and appropriate, in the following order and format. Each bulleted element here should be separated by a period. If no other formatting (quotation marks, underlining, etc.) is specified, then none should be added.

- **The name of the author or editor,** last name first for the first author or editor listed. Names of additional authors or others listed, anywhere in the entry, should appear in the regular order (first name first). (Multiple authors or editors should be listed in the order in which they appear on the book's title page. Use initials or middle names, just as they appear. You need not include titles, affiliations, and any academic degrees that precede or follow names.)
- **Title of a part of a book,** in quotation marks. Needed only if you cite a chapter, introduction, or other part of a book written by someone other than the principal author or editor listed on the title page. See "A work in an anthology or a compilation," "An article in a reference work," or "An introduction, preface, foreword, or afterword" on the following pages.
- **The title of the book,** italicized. If there is a subtitle, put a colon after the main title, and follow this with the full subtitle. This is the standard format for a works cited entry, even if there is no colon on the book's title page. (If the main title ends in a question mark, an exclamation point, or a dash, however, do not add a colon between the main title and subtitle.)
- **Name of the editor** (for books with both an author and an editor), **translator,** or **compiler,** if different from the primary author(s), with the abbreviation *Ed.*, *Trans.*, or *Comp.*, as appropriate.
- **Edition used,** if other than the first.
- **Volume used,** if a multivolume work.

(handwritten margin notes: "keep a list of all of them"; "list all the possible titles")

- **City or place of publication,** followed by a colon (if more than one city is listed on the title page, use only the first one); **name of the publisher,** followed by a comma; **year of publication** (if multiple copyright dates are listed, use the most recent one).
- **Page numbers.** Needed only if you cite a chapter, introduction, or other part of a book written by someone other than the principal author or editor listed on the title page. See "A work in an anthology or a compilation," "An article in a reference work," or "An introduction, preface, foreword, or afterword" on the following pages.
- **Medium of publication,** such as Print, Web, CD, DVD, Film, Lecture, Performance, Radio, Television, or E-mail.
- **Series name,** if the book is part of a series.

Copy your entries directly from the book's title page, which provides more complete and accurate information than a cover or another bibliography. The following examples cover most of the sorts of books you are likely to encounter.

A book by a single author. The simplest entry is a single-volume book by a single author, not part of a series, and without additional editors, translators, etc.

> Alexie, Sherman. *The Absolutely True Diary of a Part-Time Indian*. New York: Little, 2007. Print.

If a book has an editor, translator, or compiler in addition to an author, identify this person by role and by name, between the book's title and the place of publication.

> Sebald, W. G. *The Rings of Saturn*. Trans. Michael Hulse. New York: New Directions, 1998. Print.

The following example cites a third-edition book by a single author.

> Richter, David H. *The Critical Tradition: Classic Texts and Contemporary Trends*. 3rd ed. Boston: Bedford, 2007. Print.

book by two or three authors. Note that in the following example only he first author's name appears in reverse order. UP (with no periods) is he abbreviation for University Press. Note also the series title, Oxford hakespeare Topics, included when citing a book in a series.

> Gurr, Andrew, and Mariko Ichikawa. *Staging in Shakespeare's Theaters*.
> Oxford: Oxford UP, 2000. Print. Oxford Shakespeare Topics.

A book by four or more authors. If there are four or more authors or editors listed on a book's title page, give only the name of the first, followed by *et al.* (Latin for "and others").

> Gardner, Janet E., et al., eds. *Literature: A Portable Anthology*. 2nd ed.
> Boston: Bedford, 2009. Print.

A book by an unknown or anonymous author.

> *Gilgamesh: A New English Version*. Trans. Stephen Mitchell. New York:
> Free, 2006. Print.

A book by a corporate author. Corporate authorship refers to a book that lists an organization rather than an individual as its author. This is especially common with publications from government and nonprofit organizations. GPO stands for the Government Printing Office, which publishes most U.S. federal documents.

I didn't know that

> Bureau of the Census. *Historical Statistics of the United States, 1789-*
> *1945: A Supplement to the Statistical Abstract of the United States*.
> Washington: GPO, 1945. Print.

Two or more books by the same author. If you cite more than one work by a single author, alphabetize the entries by title. For the second and all subsequent entries by the same author, replace the author's name with three hyphens.

I didn't know that either.

> Bloom, Harold. *Hamlet: Poem Unlimited*. New York: Riverhead-Penguin,
> 2003. Print.
>
> ---. *Shakespeare's Poems and Sonnets*. Bloom's Major Poets. Broomall:
> Chelsea, 1999. Print.

A work in an anthology or compilation. The first example that follows i a citation from a literature anthology; the second is from a scholarly wor in which each chapter is written by a different author. The title of the wor or chapter being cited is usually enclosed in quotation marks. However, the piece is a play or novel, you should italicize its title instead.

Baldwin, James. "Sonny's Blues." *Literature: A Portable Anthology*. Ed.
   Janet E. Gardner et al. 2nd ed. Boston: Bedford, 2009. 250-76. Print.

Keyishian, Harry. "Shakespeare and the Movie Genre: The Case of
   Hamlet." *The Cambridge Companion to Shakespeare on Film*.
   Ed. Russell Jackson. Cambridge: Cambridge UP, 2000. 72-81. Print.

Two or more works in a single anthology or compilation. If you cite two
or more works from a single anthology or collection, you can create a
cross-reference, citing the full publication information for the collection
as a whole and cross-referencing the individual pieces using only the
name of the editor and page numbers of the particular work within the
anthology or compilation.

Chopin, Kate. "The Story of an Hour." Gardner et al. 66-68.

Gardner, Janet E., et al., eds. *Literature: A Portable Anthology*. 2nd ed.
   Boston: Bedford, 2009. Print.

Gilman, Charlotte Perkins. "The Yellow Wallpaper." Gardner et al. 70-83.

An article in a reference work. The format for citing material from
dictionaries, encyclopedias, or other specialized reference works is
similar to that for a work in an anthology, but the name of the reference
work's editor is omitted. Often, such reference articles are anonymous
anyway. The first example is for a signed article in a print book, the
second for an anonymous entry in an electronic encyclopedia.

Brown, Andrew. "Sophocles." *The Cambridge Guide to Theatre*. Cambridge:
   Cambridge UP, 1988. 899-900. Print.

"Browning, Elizabeth Barrett." *Encyclopaedia Britannica Online*.
   Encyclopaedia Britannica, 2008. Web. 4 Feb. 2008.

An introduction, preface, foreword, or afterword. After the author's
name, give the name of the part of the book being cited, capitalized but
neither underlined nor in quotation marks, followed by the title of the
book and all relevant publication information.

Bode, Carl. Introduction. *The Portable Thoreau*. By Henry David
   Thoreau. Ed. Bode. Revised ed. Harmondsworth, Eng.: Penguin,
   1977. 1-27. Print. Viking Portable Library.

Citing Periodicals

An article in a scholarly journal. Most scholarly journals publish several issues in each annual volume and paginate continuously throughout the entire volume. (In other words, if one issue ends on page 230, the next will begin with page 231.) Your works cited entry should list the author, article title, journal title, volume number (in arabic numerals, even if it appears in roman numeral form on the journal cover), the issue number, the year (in parentheses), and page numbers. Follow the punctuation shown here exactly.

> Miller, Greg. "The Bottom of Desire in Suzan-Lori Parks's *Venus*." *Modern Drama* 45.1 (2002): 125-37. Print.

If the journal you are citing paginates each issue separately, you must also include the issue number.

> Orban, Clara. "Antonioni's Women, Lost in the City." *Modern Language Studies* 31.2 (2001): 11-27. Print.

An article in a magazine. For an article in a magazine, omit the volume and issue numbers (if given) and include the date of publication. The first example here shows the format for a monthly, bimonthly, or quarterly magazine; the second, which includes the date as well as the month, is appropriate for weekly and biweekly magazines.

> McChesney, Robert W., and John Nichols. "Holding the Line at the FCC." *Progressive* Apr. 2003: 26-29. Print.

> Welch, Jilly. "Campaign Spells Out Concern for Literacy." *People Management* 18 Apr. 1996: 6-7. Print.

An article in a newspaper. When a newspaper is separated into **sections**, note the letter or number designating the section as a part of the page reference. Newspapers and some magazines frequently place articles on **nonconsecutive pages**. When this happens, give the number of the first page only, followed by the plus sign. For locally published newspapers, state the city of the publication if not included in the paper's name. Do this by adding the city in square brackets after the newspaper's name: *Argus Leader* [Sioux Falls]. If the masthead notes a specific edition, add a comma after the date and list the edition (for example, *natl. ed.*, *late ed.*). Different editions of the same issue of a newspaper contain different material, so it's important to note which edition you are using.

Mahren, Elizabeth. "University's 'Leap of Faith' Becomes Lesson
in Community." *Los Angeles Times* 16 Mar. 2003: A1+. Print.

A review. To cite a review, you must include the title and author of the work being reviewed between the review title and the periodical title. The *Oh ~* first entry that follows is for a book review in a magazine. The second is an untitled review in a scholarly journal that includes the name of an adaptor as well as the place and date of the play's production.

Ilan Stavans. "Familia Faces." Rev. of *Caramelo*, by Sandra Cisneros.
Nation 10 Feb. 2003: 30-34. Print.

Sofer, Andrew. Rev. of *Lysistrata*, by Aristophanes. Adapt. Robert
Brustein. Amer. Repertory Theatre, Cambridge, 28 May 2002.
Theater Journal 55.1 (2003): 137-38. Print.

Citing Electronic Sources

found that out the hard way...

Sometimes online sources do not list all the information required for a complete citation. They are, for instance, frequently anonymous, and they do not always record the dates when they were written or updated. Give as much of the information as you can find, using the formats that follow. Note that entries for online sources generally contain two dates. The first is the date when the document was posted or updated; the second is the date the researcher accessed the document.

A CD-ROM. An entry for a CD-ROM resembles a book entry, with the addition of the acronym *CD-ROM* inserted at the end as the medium of publication.

Shakespeare: His Life, Times, Works, and Sources. Princeton: Films for the
Humanities and Sciences, 1995. CD-ROM.

An online scholarly project or database. A full entry for an online scholarly project or database includes the editor's name; the title of the project, italicized; the name of the sponsoring organization or institution; the date of the project's most recent update; the medium; and the date that you accessed the project.

Folsom, Ed, and Kenneth M. Price, eds. *The Walt Whitman Archive*. Walt
Whitman Archive. 2009. Web. 1 Apr. 2009. *← date accessed.*

An online journal or magazine. The first entry that follows is from an
online scholarly journal that does not have issue numbers or page
numbers, the second is from the online version of a popular magazine.

Fukuda, Tatsuaki. "Faulknerian Topography." *The Faulkner Journal of
Japan*. 4 (2002): n. pag. Web. 20 Mar. 2003.

Keegan, Rebecca Winters. "Redeeming Roman Polanski." *Time*. Time Inc.
24 Jan. 2008. Web. 4 Feb. 2008.

A professional or personal Web page. Include as much of the following
information as appropriate and available: the author of the document or
site; the document title, in quotation marks (if the site is divided into
separate documents); the name of the site, italicized; the sponsoring
organization or institution; the date of creation or most recent update; the
medium; and your date of access. If the site has no official title, provide a
brief identifying phrase, neither underlined nor in quotation marks, as in
the second example below.

[handwritten: That's a lot to get down!]

Werner, Liz. "A Brief History of the Dickinson Homestead." *The Dickinson
Homestead: Home of Emily Dickinson*. Amherst Coll., 2001. Web.
12 June 2003.

Korista, Kirk. Home page. Western Michigan U, 3 June 2008. Web. 20 Oct.
2008.

A blog.

Curran, Kevin. "The Newspaper and the Culture of Print in the Early
American Republic." *Textual Studies, 1500–1800*, 7 Jan. 2008.
Web. 14 Jan. 2008.

A wiki.

"Cornelius Eady." *Wikipedia*. Wikimedia Foundation, 7 Apr. 2009. Web. 20
Apr. 2009.

An e-book.

> Enterline, Lynn. *The Rhetoric of the Body from Ovid to Shakespeare.*
> Cambridge: Cambridge UP, 2000. *Northwestern University Ebrary.*
> Web. 30 Nov. 2007.

A posting to a discussion list or newsgroup. Give the author's name, the title of the posting (in quotation marks) taken from the subject line, the title of the site on which the forum is found (no special formatting), the sponsor of the site, the date of posting, the medium, and your date of access. If the posting has no title, the identifying phrase *Online posting.*

[handwritten: what is you can't find it?]

> Arnove, Anthony. "Query Regarding Arthur Miller." *Campaign against*
> *Sanctions on Iraq.* Iraq Analysis Group, 28 Jan. 2000. Web.
> 20 Apr. 2003.

Citing Other Miscellaneous Sources

A television or radio program. Begin with the name of the author or another individual (director, narrator, etc.), only if you refer primarily to the work of a particular individual. Otherwise, begin with the title of a segment or episode (if appropriate), in quotation marks; the title of the program, italicized; the title of the series (if applicable), italicized; the name of the network; the call letters and city of the local station (if applicable), the date of broadcast, and the medium. The first entry that follows is a citation of a segment of a radio broadcast, the second is of an episode of a television program.

> Alison, Jay. "For Sale." *This American Life.* Public Radio Intl. WCAI,
> Woods Hole, MA, 11 Oct. 2002. Radio.

> "The Undertaking." *Frontline.* WGBH, Boston, 30 Oct. 2007. Television.

A film, video, or DVD. Film citations begin with the film title (underlined), followed by *Dir.* and the director's name, the year the film was originally released, the distributor, the year of release, and the medium (Videocassette, DVD, etc.).

[handwritten: that's actually really helpful]

> *Hamlet.* Dir. Laurence Olivier. 1948. Home Vision Entertainment, 2000. DVD.

An interview. Begin with the name of the person interviewed. For a published interview, give the title, if any, in quotation marks (if there is no title, simply use the designation *Interview*, neither in quotation marks nor italicized), followed by the name of the interviewer, publication information, and medium. The first example that follows is for an interview published in a magazine. The second example is of an interview conducted personally by the author of the research paper and gives the name of the person interviewed.

> Shields, David. "The Only Way Out Is Deeper In." Interview by
>   Andrew C. Gottlieb. *Poets & Writers* July/Aug. 2002: 27-31. Print.

> Smith, Stephen. Personal interview. 20 Mar. 2002.

A lecture or speech. To cite a speech or lecture that you've attended, use the following format, listing the speaker's name; the title of the presentation, in quotation marks (if announced or published); the sponsoring organization; the location; the date and a descriptive label such as *Address* or *Lecture*. The first example given here is for a speech with an announced title. The second is for an untitled address.

> Cohen, Amy R. "Sharing the Orchestra: How Modern Productions Reveal
>   Ancient Conventions." Sixth Natl. Symposium on Theater in Academe.
>   Washington and Lee U, Lexington, VA. 15 Mar. 2003. Speech.

> Nader, Ralph. U of Massachusetts Dartmouth, North Dartmouth. 24 Mar.
>   2003. Address.

To cite a lecture, speech, or address you've seen in a film or TV broadcast or heard on the radio, use the appropriate format for the medium of transmission. Generally speaking, you do not need to cite a class lecture; to quote or otherwise refer to something an instructor says in class, you may do so simply by crediting the instructor in the text of your essay.

A letter or e-mail. There are three kinds of letters: published, unpublished (in archives), and personal. A published letter includes the writer's name, the recipient's name (in quotation marks), the date of the letter, the number of the letter (if assigned by the editor), and publication information for the book or periodical in which it appears.

> Thomas, Dylan. "To Donald Taylor." 28 Oct. 1944. *Dylan Thomas: The
>   Collected Letters.* Ed. Paul Ferris. New York: Macmillan, 1985.
>   529-30. Print.

In citing an unpublished letter, give the writer's name, the title or a description of the material (for example, *Letter to Havelock Ellis*), the date, the medium (*MS* for a handwritten letter, *TS* for a letter composed on a machine), and any identifying number assigned to it. Include the name and location of the library or institution housing the material.

> Sanger, Margaret. Letter to Havelock Ellis. 14 July 1924. MS. Margaret
> Sanger Papers. Sophia Smith Collection. Smith Coll.,
> Northampton, MA.

To cite a letter you received personally, include the author, the designation *Letter to the author*, the date posted, and the medium (*MS* for a handwritten letter, *TS* for a letter composed on a machine). To cite an e-mail you received personally, include the author, the designation *Message to the author*, the date of the message, and the designation *E-mail*.

> Green, Barclay. Letter to the author. 1 Sept. 2002. TS.

> Kapadia, Parmita. Message to the author. 12 Mar. 2003. E-mail.

SAMPLE RESEARCH PAPER

When choosing a research paper topic, Jarrad Nunes recalled how interesting he had found Emily Dickinson's poem "Because I could not stop for Death," which seemed to defy his expectations of literature about death and dying. (If you do not know this famous poem, you can find it on the World Wide Web easily.) Jarrad decided to see what professional literary critics had to say on the subject and how closely their ideas matched his own. His paper, which follows, is a type of **reader-response criticism**, because it attends to reader expectations and how Dickinson manipulates these, and it combines a close reading of the primary literary text with research from a variety of secondary sources.

Jarrad S. Nunes

English 204

Professor Gardner

2 April 2008

Emily Dickinson's "Because I could

not stop for Death":

Challenging Readers' Expectations

With a keen eye for detail and a steadfast "resilience not to

be overcome by mysteries that eluded religion, science, and the

law" (Eberwein 42), Emily Dickinson's poetry records the abstrac-

tions of human life so matter-of-factly that her readers often

take her technical skill for granted. Take, for example, the six-

stanza poem "Because I could not stop for Death" — a detached,

but never completely dispassionate, recollection of a human's

journey to its final conclusion. The verse is crafted so succinctly

and with such precision that its complex and vivid images are

made even more extraordinary and meaningful. We might expect

literature on the theme of death to invoke religious imagery,

stillness, and a sense of dread or foreboding, but none of this

is the case. Instead, the poem challenges the preconceptions

Dickinson's contemporaries had about death, and in doing so it

makes us challenge ours as well.

   From the start, Dickinson infuses this often-grim topic with

a palpable humanity, beginning with her personification of death

as the courteous, careful carriage driver bearing the narrator's

body to rest. Literary critic Harold Bloom asserts, "The image

here of a woman and her escort, Death, meditating on the

prospect of eternity, is neither one of despair nor loss nor out-

rage, but of resignation" (37). This "resignation," though, does

not come across as the predictable acceptance of God's will. In

fact, any mention of God or the soul is remarkably absent from

this poem about death and eternity. This suggests the uneasy

relationship Dickinson had with the strict religious beliefs of her

Jarrad focu
on one Dic
poem.

Because
mention
Bloom
beginni
sentenc
does n
include
name
text ci

society and her family. "Raised during the period of New England Revivalism," writes David Yezzi, "Dickinson declined to make the public confession of faith that would admit her to the church (her father made his twice) and by the age of thirty she left off attending services altogether." Clearly at odds with familial and social expectations, Dickinson nonetheless fearlessly expresses her religious "doubt, which her poems later absorbed as ambiguity and contradiction" (Yezzi).

Jarrad integrates Yezzi's quotation with his own writing in order to provide some cultural context.

Dickinson's narrator does not fear death, perhaps because death is associated here not so much with endings or divine judgment but instead with a very human journey. The driver seems affable, "kindly stopp[ing]" and driving slowly. In stanza two, the narrator puts her work away to observe the driver calmly. It may seem unlikely that she would be trusting of so ominous a character, but as Thomas Johnson explains it:

> Emily Dickinson envisions Death as a person she knew and trusted, or believed that she could trust. He might be any Amherst gentleman, a William Howland or an Elbridge Bowdoin, or any of the lawyers or teachers or ministers whom she remembered from her youth, with whom she had exchanged valentines, and who at one time or another had acted as her squire. (222)

Jarrad indents this long quotation to set it apart from his own prose.

Indeed, the fact that the carriage driver has stopped for the narrator on a day when she was too busy to do the same emphasizes his courtesy and thoughtfulness as a character. This is an original and deeply humanistic perception of death, in which the personified entity is neither a black-cloaked grim reaper nor a stern servant of God.

Along with its deep humanity, Dickinson's image of Death has a fluidity and graceful movement that is, at first, juxtaposed against our more frightening preconceptions of the idea. This tangible sense of motion is perhaps best illustrated in the poem's perfectly constructed third stanza. Here, a series of images metaphorically re-creates a natural progression — childish play gives way to growing grain, and, eventually, to the setting of the sun (lines 9-12). At least one critic has pointed out how these three images might represent childhood, maturity, and old age (Shaw 20). The very fact that the narrator views these scenes from a slowly rolling carriage lends the passage a clear sense of movement and an unexpected vitality. The absurdity of this meandering vessel passing "the Setting Sun" perhaps suggests a sense of quickening as death draws near, or it may even signal the dissolution of temporal reality altogether. Regardless, the steady progression of this section is undeniable.

Jarrad para-phrases Shaw point in his ow words, then provides an appropriate in-text citatio

The strong sense of motion is continued in the fourth stanza, though with some differences. Here, the movement is less concrete, as the narrator herself moves from a life marked by careful self-control into a position in which she all but succumbs to outside forces. As "the Dews drew quivering and chill" (14), the narrator has lost the ability to keep herself warm. Her earthly garments do not provide adequate protection. From her philo-sophical viewpoint, however, these difficulties, like death itself, are to be calmly accepted rather than feared. Indeed, up to this point, there is not a single truly fearful image in this remarkable poem about death.

Jarrad's sm transition p vides a link between his analyses of stanzas.

As the poem moves into its fifth stanza, the momentum is halted temporarily and a more traditional death image is finally introduced with the lines "We paused before a House that seemed / A Swelling of the Ground" (17-18). At this point, the character of Death seems to bid his passenger a rather unceremonial goodbye at the foot of her earthen grave. As the resting place is described, he retreats, returning to the world of the living to repeat his duty with another passenger. While the sparse but vivid description of the grave should invoke a paralyzing loneliness, Dickinson again thwarts our expectations, tempering the reader's fear by having her narrator merely pause at the sight, as if staying for a short

Jarrad co tently ch importar tions fro poem as for his o

while at a hotel or a friend's house. Once again, a usual symbol of finality is given a transitive purpose.

The final stanza seemingly places the narrator at a new destination, Eternity. While this would certainly be the logical end of her journey, Dickinson's exquisite use of language suggests that the entire account may simply be a daydream — a mental dress rehearsal for the real death to come. Consider this account of the poem's final stanza:

> All of this poetically elapsed time "Feels shorter than the Day," the day of death brought to an end by the setting sun of the third stanza. . . . "Surmised," carefully placed near the conclusion, is all the warranty one needs for reading this journey as one that has taken place entirely in her mind . . . the poem returns to the very day, even the same instant, when it started.
> (Anderson 245)

Thus even the most basic facts about death — its finality and permanence — are brought into question.

Finally, "Because I could not stop for Death" indicates both Dickinson's precise and vivid style and her unwillingness to settle for the ordinary interpretation. Death no longer conforms to the readers' preconceptions, as religion, stillness, and finality give way to humanist philosophy, motion, and continuity. The poet observes, experiences, and recounts her perceptions in metaphor. She opens up many questions about the nature of death, yet she provides no easy answers to her readers. Instead, we are provided with an account of death that weaves in and out of time, finally looping back on its own structure to provide a stunningly dramatic conclusion. In six short stanzas, Dickinson cleverly exposes what she saw as fundamental flaws in the traditional conception of death, burial, and the eternal afterlife, and in doing so, she opens up new pathways of thought for us all.

In his conclusion, Jarrad reinforces his claim: that the poem challenges nineteenth-century notions of death.

Works Cited

Anderson, Charles R. *Emily Dickinson's Poetry: Stairway of Surprise*.
New York: Holt, 1960. Print.

Bloom, Harold. *Emily Dickinson*. New York: Chelsea, 1999. Print.   *Book in a series*
Bloom's Major Poets.

Dickinson, Emily. "Because I could not stop for Death."   *A poem reprint*
Literature: A Portable Anthology. Ed. Janet E. Gardner   *in an antholog*
et al. 2nd ed. Boston: Bedford, 2009. 537. Print.

Eberwein, Jane Donahue. "Dickinson's Local, Global, and Cosmic   *A selection fro*
Perspectives." *The Emily Dickinson Handbook*. Ed. Gudrun   *an edited boo*
Grabher. Amherst: U of Massachusetts P, 1998. 27-43. Print.

Johnson, Thomas. *Emily Dickinson: An Interpretive
Biography*. Cambridge: Harvard UP, 1955. Print.

Shaw, Mary Neff. "Dickinson's 'Because I could not stop for
Death.'" *Explicator* 50 (1991): 20-21. Print.

Yezzi, David. "Straying Close to Home." *Commonweal*. Commonweal   *An online ve*
Foundation, 9 Oct. 1998. Web. 20 May 2009.   *of a magazi*
        article.

o include Sownes you've closely read (not exactly cited though)

o include all Sownes used.

CHAPTER 8

Literary Criticism and Literary Theory

Anytime you sit down to write about literature, or even to discuss a story, play, or poem with classmates, you are acting as a literary critic. The word *criticism* is often interpreted as negative and faultfinding. But literary criticism is a discipline and includes everything from a glowing review to a scathing attack to a thoughtful and balanced interpretation. Criticism can be broken down into two broad categories: **evaluative** and **interpretive**. Evaluative criticism seeks to determine how accomplished a work is and what place it should hold in the evolving story of literary history. Book reviews are the most common form of evaluative criticism. Interpretive criticism comprises all writing that seeks to explain, analyze, clarify, or question the meaning and significance of literature. Although you may engage in a certain amount of evaluative criticism in your literature class, and while your attitude about the value of literature will likely be apparent in your writing, the criticism you write for class will consist largely of interpretation.

All literary critics, including you, begin with some form of literary theory. Just as you may not have thought of yourself as a literary critic, you probably haven't thought of yourself as using literary theory. But you are doing so every time you write about literature, and it is a good idea to become familiar with some of the most prevalent types of theory. This familiarity will help you understand why so many respected literary critics seem to disagree with one another and why they write such different analyses of the same work of literature. It may also help to explain why you might disagree with your classmates, or even your instructor, in your interpretation of a particular story, poem, or play. Perhaps you are simply starting from a different theoretical base. You will be able to explain your thinking more eloquently if you understand that base.

Literary theory has the reputation of being incredibly dense and difficult. Indeed, the theories—sometimes called *schools* of criticism—discussed in the following pages are all complex, but here they are presented in their most basic, stripped-down forms. As such, these explanations are necessarily incomplete and selective. You should not feel you need to master the complexities of literary theory right now. You need only be aware of the existence of these various schools and watch for them as you read and write. Doing so will give you a better sense of what you're reading and hearing about the literature you explore, and it will make your writing more informed and articulate. There are many other schools and subschools in addition to those described here, but these are the most significant—the ones you are most likely to encounter as you continue to explore literature.

FORMALISM AND NEW CRITICISM

For a large part of the twentieth century, literary criticism was dominated by various types of theory that can broadly be defined as **formalism** and **New Criticism**. (New Criticism is no longer new, having begun to fall out of prominence in the 1970s, but its name lives on.) Formalist critics focus their attention, unsurprisingly, on the formal elements of a literary text—things like **structure**, **tone**, **characters**, **setting**, **symbols**, and linguistic features. Explication and close reading (explained on pages 1220–21) are techniques of formalist criticism. While poetry, which is most self-consciously formal in its structure, lends itself most obviously to formalist types of criticism, prose fiction and drama are also frequently viewed through this lens.

Perhaps the most distinguishing feature of formalism and New Criticism is that they focus on the text itself and not on extratextual factors. Formalist critics are interested in how parts of a text relate to one another and to the whole, and they seek to create meaning by unfolding and examining these relationships. Excluded from consideration are questions about the author, the reader, history or culture, and the relationship of the literary text to other texts or artwork. Chances are you have written some formalist criticism yourself, either in high school or in college. If you have ever written a paper on **symbolism**, *character development*, or the relationship between sound patterns and sense in a poem, you have been a formalist critic.

FEMINIST AND GENDER CRITICISM

Have you ever had a classroom discussion of a piece of literature in which the focus was on the roles of women in the literature or the culture, or on the relationships between men and women? If so, you have engaged in feminist criticism. Some version of feminist criticism has been around for as long as readers have been interested in gender roles but the school rose to prominence in the 1970s, at the same time as the modern feminist movement was gaining steam. Most **feminist criticism** from this time was clearly tied to raising consciousness about the patriarchy in which many women felt trapped. Some feminist critics sought to reveal how literary texts demonstrated the repression and powerlessness of women in different periods and cultures. Others had a nearly opposite agenda, showing how female literary characters could overcome the sexist power structures that surround them and exercise power in their worlds. Still others looked to literary history and sought to rediscover and promote writing by women whose works had been far less likely than men's to be regarded as "great" literature.

It was not long, however, before some critics began to point out that women were not alone in feeling social pressure to conform to gender roles. Over the years, men have usually been expected to be good providers, to be strong (both physically and emotionally), and to keep their problems and feelings more or less to themselves. Though the expectations are different, men are socialized no less than women to think and behave in certain ways, and these social expectations are also displayed in works of literature. Feminist criticism has expanded in recent years to become **gender criticism**. Any literary criticism that highlights gender roles or relationships between the sexes can be a type of gender criticism, whether or not it is driven by an overt feminist agenda.

MARXIST CRITICISM

Just as feminist criticism came into its own because of the political agenda of certain critics, so too did **Marxist criticism**, which originally sought to use literature and criticism to forward a socialist political program. Early Marxist critics began with Karl Marx's (1818–1883) insistence that human interactions are economically driven and that the basic model of human progress is based on a struggle for power between different social classes. For Marxist critics, then, literature was just another battleground, another venue for the ongoing quest for individual material gain. Literary characters could be divided into powerful oppressors and their powerless victims, and literary plots and themes could be examined to uncover the economic forces that drove them. According to this model, the very acts of writing and reading literature can be characterized as production and consumption, and some Marxist critics have studied the external forces that drive education, publication, and literary tastes.

The sort of Marxist criticism that ignores all forces but those that are socioeconomic is sometimes referred to as *vulgar* Marxism because, in its single-mindedness, it ignores certain complexities of individual thought and action. Its sole purpose is to expose the inequalities that underlie all societies and to thus raise the consciousness of readers and move society closer to a socialist state. Such Marxist criticism tends to be full of the language of Marxist political analysis—references to *class struggle*, to the economic *base* and *superstructure*, to the *means of production*, to worker *alienation* and *reification* (the process whereby oppressed workers lose their sense of individual humanity), and so forth.

But just as feminist criticism soon opened up into the broader and more complex school of gender criticism, so too did some Marxist criticism break free of a single-minded political agenda. You no longer have to be a committed Marxist to engage in Marxist criticism; all you need to do is acknowledge that socioeconomic forces do, in fact, affect people's lives. If you notice inequalities in power between characters in a work of literature, if you question how the class or educational background of an author affects his or her work, or if you believe that a certain type of literature—a Shakespearean sonnet, say, or a pulp Western novel— appeals more to readers of a particular social background, then you are, at least in part, engaging in Marxist criticism.

CULTURAL STUDIES

Cultural studies is the general name given to a wide variety of critical practices, some of which might seem on the surface to have little in common with one another. Perhaps the best way to understand cultural studies is to begin with the notion that certain texts are privileged in our society while others are dismissed or derided. Privileged texts are the so-called great works of literature one commonly finds in anthologies and on course syllabi. Indeed, when we hear the word *literature*, these are probably the works we imagine. All other writing—from pulp romance novels to the slogans on bumper-stickers—belong to a second category of texts, those generally overlooked by traditional literary critics.

One major trend in cultural studies is the attempt to broaden the **canon**—those texts read and taught again and again and held up as examples of the finest expressions of the human experience. Critics have pointed out that canonical authors—Shakespeare, Milton, Keats, Steinbeck—tend (with obvious exceptions) to be from a fairly narrow segment of society: they are usually middle to upper-middle class, well-educated, heterosexual white males. Some cultural critics, therefore, have sought out and celebrated the writing of historically disadvantaged groups such as African Americans or gay and lesbian authors. One very active branch of cultural studies is **postcolonial criticism**, which focuses on writing from former British (and other) colonies around the world, where local authors often display attitudes and tastes very different from those of their former colonial masters. Other branches of cultural studies turn their attention to the works of various social "outsiders," like prisoners, school children, or mental patients. This attempt at broadening the canon is designed to provide students and scholars alike with a more inclusive definition of what art and literature are all about.

Cultural critics seek to blur or erase the line separating "high" from "low" art in the minds of the literary establishment. Some cultural critics believe that all texts are to some extent artistic expressions of a culture, and that any text can therefore give us vital insights into the human experience. Rather than traditional literary objects, then, a cultural critic might choose to study such things as movies and television shows, advertisements, religious tracts, graffiti, and comic books. These texts—and virtually any other visual or verbal work you can imagine—are submitted to the same rigorous scrutiny as a sonnet or a classic novel. Some cultural critics suggest that English departments should become departments of cultural studies, in which a course on hiphop culture would be valued as much as a course on Victorian poetry.

HISTORICAL CRITICISM AND NEW HISTORICISM

If you have ever written a research paper that involved some background reading about the life and times of an author, you have already engaged in a form of **historical criticism**. Literary scholars have long read history books and various sorts of historical documents—from newspaper articles to personal letters—to gain insights into the composition and significance of a given work. The explanatory footnotes that often appear in literary reprints and anthologies are one obvious manifestation of this type of sleuthing. Indeed, a work of literature could be virtually inexplicable if we did not understand something of the times in which it was written and first read. If you did not know that Walt Whitman's "When Lilacs Last in the Dooryard Bloom'd" was an elegy written upon the assassination of Abraham Lincoln, it would be difficult to make any sense at all of the poem, since neither the president's name nor the cause of his death actually appear in the work.

Likewise, historians have long turned to literary works and the visual arts in order to gain insights into the periods they study. While archives and contemporary documents can teach us a lot about the broad sweep of history—wars, leaders, the controversies of the day—it is often difficult to see from these documents what life was like for ordinary people, whose interior lives were not often documented. We may be able to learn from parish burial records, for example, how common childhood mortality was at a particular time in English history, but only when we read Ben Jonson's poem "On My First Son" do we begin to understand how this mortality may have affected the parents who lost their children. Likewise, the few pages of James Joyce's story "Araby" may tell us more about how adolescent boys lived and thought in turn-of-the-century Dublin than several volumes of social history.

One school of historical criticism, known as **New Historicism**, takes account of both what history has to teach us about literature *and* what literature has to teach us about history. (New Historicism has been around since the 1960s, and as with New Criticism, the name of the school is no longer as accurate as it once was.) New Historicists are sometimes said to read literary and nonliterary texts *in parallel*, attempting to see how each illuminates the other. Typically, New Historicists will examine many different types of documents—government records, periodicals, private diaries, bills of sale—in order to re-create, as much as possible, the rich cultural context that surrounded both an author and that author's original audience. In doing so, they seek to give modern audiences a reading experience as rich and informed as the original readers of a literary work.

PSYCHOLOGICAL THEORIES

At the beginning of the twenty-first century, it is easy to underestimate the enormous influence that the theories of the psychoanalyst Sigmund Freud (1856–1939) have had on our understanding of human behavior and motivation. For many modern readers, Freud seems to have little to say; his work is too focused on sex and too thoroughly bound by the norms of the bourgeois Viennese society in which he lived. But if you have ever wondered what the buried significance of a dream was or whether someone had a subconscious motivation for an action, you have been affected by Freudian thinking. Freud popularized the notions that the mind can be divided into conscious and unconscious components and that we are often motivated most strongly by the unconscious. He taught us to think in terms of overt and covert desires (often referred to in Freudian language as *manifest* and *latent*) as the basis of human actions.

Like many intellectual movements of the twentieth century, psychology, and specifically Freudian psychology, has had a major influence on literary criticism. The most typical **psychological literary criticism** examines the internal mental states, the desires, and the motivations of literary characters. (In fact, Freud himself used Shakespeare's Hamlet as an example of a man whose life was ruled by what the psychiatrist called an Oedipal complex—man's unhealthy, but not uncommon, interest in his mother's sexuality.) Another subject of psychological criticism can be the author. A critic may examine the possible unconscious urges that drove an author to write a particular story or poem. Finally, a critic might examine the psychology of readers, trying to determine what draws us to or repels us from certain literary themes or forms. If any of these aspects of literature have ever interested you, you have engaged in psychological literary criticism.

Psychological critics often interpret literature as a psychologist might interpret a dream or a wish. Special attention is often paid to symbols as the manifest representation of a deeper, hidden meaning. Attention is also focused on the unstated motives and unconscious states of mind of characters, authors, or readers. Freud is not the only psychological theorist whose ideas are frequently used in literary analysis. Other important figures include Carl Jung (1875–1961), who gave us the notion of the collective unconscious and the influence of **archetypes** on our thinking, and Jacques Lacan (1901–1981), who had a special interest in the unconscious and the nature of language. You don't, however, need to be well-versed in the intricacies of psychoanalytic theory in order to be interested in the inner workings of the human mind or the ways in which they manifest themselves in literature.

READER-RESPONSE THEORIES

You no doubt have heard the old question: If a tree falls in the forest and nobody hears it, did the tree make a sound? Let us rephrase that question: If a book sits on a shelf and nobody reads it, what effect does the book have on the world? If you use **reader-response criticism**, your answer to that question will be a resounding *none*. Of course, the book exists as a physical object, a sheaf of paper bound in a cover and printed with symbols. But, say reader-response critics, as a work of art or a conduit for meaning, no text exists without a reader.

A text, according to the various theories of reader-response criticism, is not a container filled with meaning by its author but rather an interaction between an author and a reader, and it can never be complete unless readers bring to it their own unique insights. These insights come from a number of sources, including the reader's life experience as well as his or her beliefs, values, state of mind at the time of the reading, and, of course, previous reading experience. Reading is not a passive attempt to understand what lies within a text but an act of creation, no less so than the writing itself. Reader-response critics try to understand the process by which we make meaning out of words on a page. If you have ever wondered why a classmate or friend saw something entirely different than you did in a story or poem, then you have been a reader-response critic.

Two key terms associated with reader-response criticisms are *gaps* and *process*. Gaps are those things that a text doesn't tell us, that we need to fill in and work out for ourselves. Let us say, for instance, that you read a story told from the perspective of a child, but the author never explicitly mentions the child's age. How, then, do you imagine the narrator as you read? You pay attention to his or her actions and thoughts, and you compare this to your experience of real children you have known and others whose stories you have read. In doing so, you fill in a *gap* in the text and help solidify the text's meaning. Imagine, though, that as the story continues, new clues emerge and you need to adjust your assumptions about the child's age. This highlights the idea that reading is a *process*, that the meaning of the text is not fixed and complete but rather evolving as the text unfolds in the time it takes to read.

Some reader-response critics focus on the ways that meanings of a text change over time. To illustrate this idea, let us look at a specific example. Contemporary readers of Kate Chopin's short novel *The Awakening*, first published in 1899, tend to find the book's treatment of the heroine's sexuality subtle or even invisible. Such readers are often shocked or amused to learn that the book was widely condemned at the time of its publication as tasteless and overly explicit. Expectations and tastes change over time and place, and we can tell a lot about a society by examining how it responds to works of art. Reader-response critics, therefore, sometimes ask us to look at our own reactions to literature and to ask how, if at all, they match up with those of earlier readers. When we look at reactions to *The Awakening* at the end of the nineteenth century and then at the beginning of the twenty-first, we learn not only about Chopin's culture but also about our own.

STRUCTURALISM

Structuralism, as the name implies, is concerned with the structures that help us to understand and interpret literary texts. This may sound like a return to formalism, which, as we saw earlier, examines the formal and linguistic elements of a text. But the elements scrutinized by structuralist critics are of a different order entirely, being the structures that order our thinking rather than the interior architecture of poems, stories, and plays. Structuralist criticism actually derives from the work of anthropologists, linguists, and philosophers of the mid-twentieth century who sought to understand how humans thought and communicated. The basic insight at the heart of the movement is the realization that w understand nothing in isolation but rather that every piece of our knowledge is part of a network of associations. Take, for instance, the question, "Is Jim a good father?" In order to form a simple yes or no answer to this question, we must consider, among other things, the spectrum of "good" and "bad," the expectations our culture holds for fathers, and all we know of Jim's relationship with his children.

For a structuralist literary critic, questions about literature are answered with the same sort of attention to context. Two different types of context are especially salient—the cultural and the literary. Cultural context refers to an understanding of all aspects of an author's (and a reader's) culture, including but not limited to the organizing structures of history, politics, religion, education, work, and family. Literary context refers to all related texts, literary and nonliterary, that affect our ability to interpret a text. What had the author read that might have affected the creation of the text? What have we read that might affect our interpretation? What are the norms of the textual genre, and how does this piece of literature conform to or break from those norms?

According to structuralist critics, then, we can only understand a text by placing it within the broader contexts of culture (that of both the reader and the author) and other texts (literary and nonliterary). To fully understand one of Shakespeare's love sonnets to the mysterious "dark lady," for example, we would need to understand the conventions of romantic love, the conceptions of dark versus fair women in culturally accepted standards of beauty, and the acceptable interactions between men and women in Shakespeare's England. We would also need to relate the sonnet to the history of love poems generally, to the development of the sonnet form specifically, and to the other works in Shakespeare's cycle of 154 sonnets.

POSTSTRUCTURALISM AND DECONSTRUCTION

Poststructuralism, it will come as no surprise, begins with the insights of structuralism but carries them one step further. If, as the structuralists insist, we can understand things only in terms of other things, then perhaps there is no center point of understanding but only an endlessly interconnected web of ideas leading to other ideas leading to still other ideas. This is the starting point of poststructuralist criticism, which posits that no text has a fixed or real meaning because no meaning exists outside of the network of other meanings to which it is connected. Meaning, then, including literary meaning, is forever shifting and altering as our understanding of the world changes. The best-known version of poststructuralism is **deconstruction**, a school of philosophy and literary criticism that first gained prominence in France and that seeks to overturn the very basis of Western philosophy by undermining the notion that reality has any stable existence.

At its worst, of course, this school of thought leads to the most slippery sort of relativism. What does it matter what I think of this poem or this play? I think what I want, you think what you want. Perhaps next week I will think something different. Who cares? Every interpretation is of equal value, and none has any real value at all. At its best, though, poststructuralist criticism can lead toward truly valuable insights into literature. It reminds us that meaning within a text is contingent on all sorts of exterior understandings; it allows for several interpretations, even contradictory interpretations, to exist simultaneously; and, by insisting that no text and no meaning is absolute, it allows for a playful approach to even the most "serious" of literary objects. Indeed, one of the recurrent themes of deconstructionist criticism is the French term *jouissance*, often translated as *bliss*, which refers to a free-spirited, almost sexual enjoyment of literary language.

Having thus briefly described deconstruction, we would do well to dispel a common misconception about the word. In recent years, many people, both within and outside of academia, have begun to use *deconstruct* as a synonym for *analyze*. You might hear, for instance, "We completely deconstructed that poem in class—I understand it much better now," or "The defense attorney deconstructed the prosecutor's argument." In both these cases, what the speaker likely means has little if anything to do with the literary critical practice of deconstruction. When we take apart a text or an argument and closely examine the parts, we are engaging not in deconstruction but in analysis.

By now you may be wondering what sort of literary critic you are. You may feel that you have been a formalist one day and a psychological critic the next. This is not surprising, and it should cause you no worry, as virtually none of these schools is mutually exclusive. Indeed, most professional critics mix and match the various schools in whatever way best suits their immediate needs. The close reading techniques of the New Critics, for instance, are frequently adopted by those who would fervently reject the New Critical stance that social and political context be excluded from consideration. If you wished to write about the social decline of Mme. Loisel in Guy de Maupassant's story "The Necklace," you might well find yourself in the position of a Marxist-feminist-New Historicist critic. That's fine. Writing with the knowledge that you are drawing from Marxism, feminism, and New Historicism, you will almost certainly write a better-organized, better-informed, and more thorough paper than you would have had you begun with no conscious basis in literary theory.

Index of Terms